BOB DYLAN'S NEW YORK

A HISTORIC GUIDE

DICK WEISSMAN

EXCELSIOR
EDITIONS

COVER PHOTO: *Civil Rights March on Washington, D.C.* closeup view of vocalists Bob Dylan, August 28, 1963. Source: U.S. National Archives and Records Administration.

AUTHOR PHOTO: Dick Weissman, c. 1960. Photo Sound Associates. From the Ronald D. Cohen Collection #20239, Southern Folklife Collection, The Wilson Library, University of North Carolina at Chapel Hill.

Published by State University of New York Press, Albany

Excelsior Editions is an imprint of State University of New York Press

For information, contact State University of New York Press, Albany, NY
www.sunypress.edu

Library of Congress Cataloging-in-Publication Data

Name: Weissman, Dick, author.
Title: Bob Dylan's New York : a historic guide / Dick Weissman.
Description: Albany : State University of New York Press, 2022. | Series:
  Excelsior editions | Includes bibliographical references and index.
Identifiers: LCCN 2022009874 | ISBN 9781438490861 (pbk. : alk paper) | ISBN
  9781438490878 (ebook)
Subjects: LCSH: Dylan, Bob, 1941—Homes and haunts—New York (State)—New
  York. | Musical landmarks—New York (State)—New York. | Manhattan (New
  York, N.Y.)—Guidebooks.
Classification: LCC ML420.D98 W47 2022 | DDC 782.42164092—dc23
LC record available at https://lccn.loc.gov/2022009874

10 9 8 7 6 5 4 3 2 1

Contents

Preface/Acknowledgments

There are hundreds of books about Bob Dylan. Many are extended discourses on his political or religious beliefs, some offer detailed analysis of the lyrics to his songs, and quite a few are biographical works. This book centers on Bob's arrival in New York and his years in Greenwich Village.

Thanks to Bob Cohen, Josh Dunson, Barry Kornfeld, Happy Traum, and Terri Thal for stories, insights, and reminiscences. Each of them hung out with Bob Dylan in his Village days, and in Happy's case during Bob's years in Woodstock. Photos not otherwise credited are from the author's collection. Special thanks to the Ralph Rinzler Folklife Archives and Collections, Diana Davies Collection, Smithsonian Center for Folklife and Cultural Heritage, and The Ronald D. Cohen Collection #20239, Southern Folklife Collection, The Wilson Library, University of North Carolina at Chapel Hill for providing many of these images. Additional thanks go to my intrepid editor, Richard Carlin.

As this book was being written, my daughter Janelle was working in New York City. The photos on her phone re-awakened many memories of people and places from my Greenwich Village days.

Dick Weissman

1

Biting the Apple in Greenwich Village

Bob Dylan got to New York City in 1961. He immediately set off for the downtown section of New York that is known as Greenwich Village. Let's start off by painting a brief picture of what awaited Mr. Bob as he wandered downtown in search of a career as a modern troubadour.

Mapping the Territory

There is no strict map that defines the New York neighborhood known as Greenwich Village. A loose definition might go like this: Fourteenth Street is the northern border of the neighborhood, and I would suggest Houston Street is the southern border (for those who are not familiar with Manhattan, Houston Street is the equivalent of Zero Street). The eastern edge of the Village, for those who are literal minded, might be Fourth Avenue or Broadway; if we wish to include the so-called East Village, we might go as far east as Avenue A or B. On its west side, Greenwich Village stretches all the way to the Hudson River.

In 1811 New York created a system of streets that ran east–west and avenues that ran north–south. At that time Greenwich Village was known as Green Village, and its residents resisted this attempt to impose order on their chaotic world. City planners then elected to bypass the Village and its strange universe of streets changing names and numbering systems and bizarre intersections like West Fourth Street crossing West Tenth Street. These streets are the same today, along with odd nooks and crannies like MacDougal Alley. Nonetheless, in general New York's avenues follow a numerical pattern from east to west starting at First Avenue and going as high as 11th Avenue; east of First Avenue they are alphabetical from west to east: Avenue A up to Avenue D. MacDougal Street is a narrow street that runs parallel to the avenues between Sixth Avenue (Avenue of the Americas) and Fifth Avenue.

Residential, Commercial, Mixtures of Both, and Visitors

Different parts of the Village are designated as residential or commercial, and there are often commercial establishments located on the ground floor of apartment buildings. An example of a business/residential mixture is the building on Mac-Dougal that housed the folk music club The Gaslight, the bar the Kettle of Fish, and apartments that were located directly above the club. These establishments were jammed with customers on the weekend, which created inevitable noise problems for renters seeking a peaceful night's sleep. Small streets and even alleys contained brownstones, row houses that were made of brown-colored sandstone.

Many of the apartments on streets like MacDougal Street were available at low cost in the 1950s, but had few amenities. Elevators in these buildings were nonexistent, air conditioning was unknown, and if furnishings were available they included little beyond a bed and a dresser. As the reader will see, Dylan himself lived in such surroundings shortly after he arrived in New York City. In those days, the real estate section of the Sunday *New York Times* was available as a separate section several days in advance. Well-informed Villagers would wait in line to get the paper and be among the first in line to answer an ad.

It was also an illegal but common custom for people to advertise apartments in the weekly *Village Voice* with verbiage like "furniture available." This meant that the apartment seeker basically had to offer a bribe to obtain the lease on a low-cost apartment. I rented an apartment in the East Village. The rent was $22.85 a month, and I recall paying over a thousand dollars for the "furniture." The apartment was a five-story walk-up with no heat and the bathtub was in the kitchen. "Heat" was available by lighting the stove in the kitchen!

Demography

By the time that Dylan got to Greenwich Village, the population included three different groups. There were Italian immigrants, who dominated the restaurant, grocery, and bar businesses; Irish immigrants, who dominated the waterfront; and a bohemian population of artists, writers, and musicians that included a mixture of various ethnic groups, including a significant Jewish segment of the population. This generalization, however, didn't always hold. For example, musicians Maria D'Amato (later Muldaur), Dick Rosmini, and John Sebastian came from Italian families and grew up in the Village with their families. Maria later joined Jim Kweskin's Jug Band, and she enjoyed a successful hit record with the novelty song "Midnight at the Oasis" in 1993. Rosmini was an excellent guitarist and banjo player who also pursued his professional interests in photography and audio engineering. Sebastian was the son of famed classical harmonica player John Sebastian. The younger Sebastian wrote many successful songs and founded the band The Lovin' Spoonful.

The Artists

Because Greenwich Village developed a culture that was rich in everything from inexpensive restaurants to specialized groceries and European-style coffeehouses, it became a very comfortable environment for all sorts of artists long before the arrival of Bob Dylan. Visual artists included Andy Warhol and his Factory, Hans Hofmann the painter and art teacher, and Hofmann's students Larry Rivers, Red Grooms, and Helen Frankenthaler. Hofmann lived in a variety of Village apartments on West Eighth, West Ninth, and East Fourth Streets.

Experimental theater thrived in the Village, at such venues as Caffe Cino, the Theatre de Lys, the Cherry Lane Theatre, the Circle in the Square, the Provincetown Playhouse, and the Cornelia Street Café. In the neighboring East Village were the Living Theatre, St. Mark's Playhouse, and La MaMa. There is also a long history of creative writers who lived in the Village. This includes Djuna Barnes, William Burroughs, E.E. Cummings, Theodore Dreiser, Lorraine Hansberry, Norman Mailer, and John Reed.

In addition to the many singer-songwriters and folk singers who we will encounter later in this book, there were many composers and musicians who lived and sometimes performed in the Village or in nearby neighborhoods. This included innovative classical composers John Cage, Morton Feldman, and Edgard Varèse. Among the jazz musicians who lived in the Village or East Village were major composer-performers Charles Mingus and Charlie (Bird) Parker. There were also several venues that featured various genres of jazz, ranging from Slugs' Saloon, the Village Vanguard, Café Bohemia, the Village Gate, Nick's, and the Half Note.

Midtown

In Midtown Manhattan much of the infrastructure of the business of music, art, and book publishing was centered. There was a string of music stores, literally back to back, on West 48th Street between Sixth and Seventh Avenues. Most of the recording studios were located midtown on the west side, and the more important and successful booking agents and personal managers of musicians were there as well. So were the music publishers, notably at the Brill Building, which was located on 49th Street, and another building at the corner of 51st Street. It became the world headquarters for early rock-and-roll hit-makers.

Before He Came to New York

Bob Dylan was born Robert Allen Zimmerman in Duluth, Minnesota, on May 24, 1941. He lived in Duluth until the age of six, when his father contracted polio and moved the family to his wife's hometown of Hibbing, Minnesota. Bob went through high school in Hibbing, and was enrolled as a student at the University of Minnesota in Minneapolis from fall 1959 until fall 1960.

During his high school days Bob played piano and guitar and performed at some high school dances, and during his time at the university he hung out in the bohemian section of Minneapolis known as Dinkytown. He became friendly with white blues singers John "Spider" Koerner, Dave "Snaker" Ray, and Tony "Little Sun" Glover. Minneapolis-based folk music fans John Pankake and Paul Nelson founded the fanzine *The Little Sandy Review* in 1959, and Bob became friendly with them and listened to many of the folk music recordings that the magazine received. Bob borrowed many of Nelson's records, sometimes without permission. In 1959 he traded his electric guitar for a Martin acoustic model and took to emulating Oklahoma-born songwriter Woody Guthrie. In 1960 Dylan quit college and set off for New York, hoping to meet Woody Guthrie and to begin a career as a professional folksinger.

WOODY GUTHRIE

1. Woody Guthrie, in 1943, with his guitar carrying the motto "This machine kills fascists." Library of Congress, Prints and Photographs Division.

Woody Guthrie was a singer-songwriter before that descriptor was known to music critics. Woody had a colorful if erratic life, performing successfully on radio on the West Coast, and recording numerous albums for Moe Asch's various record labels. Woody wrote a number of "protest-y" songs, quite a few children's songs, and other songs that didn't necessarily take a specific point of view. In Minneapolis, Dylan had listened to Woody's records, and had read his fictionalized autobiography, *Bound for Glory*. Guthrie's greatest influence on the young Dylan was probably through his sense of irony; for example, in his song about the gangster "Pretty Boy Floyd," Woody says "some will rob you with a pistol, and some with a fountain pen."

By the time Bob Dylan got to New York, Guthrie was diagnosed with the neurological ailment known as Huntington's Disease. This required him to be hospitalized at Greystone Park State Hospital in Morris Plains, New Jersey. Bob took a bus to the hospital to meet the singer, where he sang Woody his own composition "Song to Woody," and in turn Woody gave Bob a card that said "I ain't dead yet."* (The Woody Guthrie Center in Tulsa sells a shirt that has the "I ain't dead yet" quote on it.) Several of Woody's family members observed that Woody seemed to have a special attachment to Bob. Bob also attempted to visit Woody's family in Brooklyn. He was searching for song lyrics that he had been advised had been left in Woody's house. Woody's ex-wife and caretaker Marjorie wasn't home when Dylan arrived, but Bob met Guthrie's daughter Nora and his young son Arlo, who went on to become a well-known songwriter and performer in his own right.

Because of Woody's illness, he served as a mentor to Bob Dylan without ever really being able to communicate. Dylan recorded several talking blues, which was a song form that Woody often used. In the talking blues form the singer talks rather than sings the lyric, with simple guitar accompaniment. Dylan famously broke his one-and-a-half-year silence following his 1966 motorcycle accident to perform at a Carnegie Hall fundraiser for Guthrie's children.

How Zimmerman Became Dylan

While in Minneapolis Bob conceived the notion of establishing a new identity for himself that was closer to the image that he wished to portray. He floated the names Elston Gunn, Robert Allin, and Bob Dillon before settling on Robert Dylan. In 1962, he legally changed his name to Bob Dylan.**

---

*Caspar Llewellyn Smith, "Bob Dylan Visits Woody Guthrie," *Guardian*, June 16, 2011, www.theguardian.com/music/2011/jun/16/bob-dylan-woody-guthrie.

**See Clinton Heylin, *The Double Life of Bob Dylan: A Restless, Hungry Feeling (1941–1966)* (New York: Little, Brown and Company, 2021).

Early Mythology

In addition to changing his name to create a new identity and mage for himself, Dylan also created a series of stories that reinforced the mystery of his upbringing. In press interviews he claimed to be an orphan who ran away from home numerous times, and said that he had traveled with a caravan and had learned how to play guitar from a one-eyed Indian in Tucson, Arizona. Folk fans were startled when it emerged that these tales were fantasies, and not facts. Blues artists such as Robert Johnson and Big Bill Broonzy and folk singer Jack Elliott similarly created identities and names and identities for themselves.

2

MacDougal Street

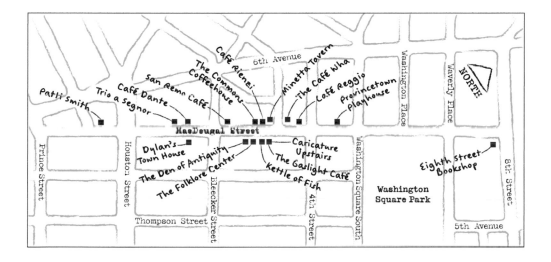

MacDougal Street is a narrow street halfway between Fifth and Sixth Avenues in the Greenwich Village section of New York City. It runs from Eighth Street on the north to Prince Street on the south. In many ways it was the main artery of the Village during its heyday from the '50s to the early to mid-'70s. Writing in 1965 in the neighborhood weekly *Village Voice,* columnist Jack Newfield describe the street's late-night scene:

> Homosexuals cruising, pill-buyers waiting, transvestites parading, and tourists watching. Aging Kerouac heroes picking up Lolitas. Black-leather-jacketed motorcyclists gunning their growling motors. High-school kids looking for a party, drunks looking for a fight. A cacophony of sound:

folk melodies prancing out of the cellars, barkers shouting their rasping pleas; taxi drivers honking their horns, the hoofbeats on asphalt of the mounted police. The mingled aromas of sausages, pizzas, horse manure and gasoline fumes.*

About the only thing left out of the description is the presence of the over 45,000 students who attended New York University by 1965, many of whom came from out of state and lived in dormitories. NYU surrounds Washington Square in virtually all directions, and MacDougal Street was a place for students seeking everything from Italian meals to the many sorts of entertainment available there or on nearby streets.

2. MacDougal Street in 1951 looking south at Third Street. Library of Congress, Prints and Photographs Division.

---

*Jack Newfield, "MacDougal at Midnight: A Street Under Pressure," *Village Voice*, April 8, 1965.

The Locations

45

Patti Smith moved to New York in 1967. As a young girl, she wrote some poems to Bob Dylan; she met him in 1974 when she was performing at the Bitter End and Dylan introduced himself to her. They later toured together in 1995. She is the current owner of the building.

77, TIRO A SEGNO ("FIRE AT THE TARGET")

This is the clubhouse of a private Italian club and rifle owners' association. It claims to be the oldest Italian heritage association in the country. Founded in 1888, the club moved to this linked group of three rowhouses originally built in the 1850s in 1924. Its members have included such noted Italian Americans as operatic superstar Enrico Caruso, mayor Fiorello LaGuardia, and auto executive Lee Iacocca. This ritzy club features what is described as a "black tie shooting range" in its basement.*

During Dylan's time in the Village, there was considerable tension between the Italian population who had lived in the Village for years and the new long-hairs who were moving in. There were several private Italian clubs in various parts of the Village, some with rumored Mafia connections.

79–81, CAFFE DANTE

Caffe Dante was opened in 1915 by Italian immigrant Mario Flotta, and still holds forth today. It was operated by him and his two sons for a hundred years. Dante was one of the many restaurant-bars in the neighborhood, and many famous Villagers have passed through its doors, including writers Anaïs Nin and Ernest Hemingway, musician Patti Smith and her good friend artist Robert Mapplethorpe, actors Alec Baldwin and Al Pacino, comedienne Whoopi Goldberg, and our own Bob Dylan. The current café uses the original name, but has nothing else in common with the original restaurant.

---

*Andrea Cihlarova, "An Underground Black Tie Shooting Range in NYC? Welcome to Tiro A Segno," *Guest of a Guest*, April 16, 2015, guestofaguest.com/new-york/nyc/an-underground-black-tie-shooting-range-in-nyc-welcome-to-tiro-a-segno.

93 (CORNER OF BLEECKER STREET), SAN REMO CAFÉ

The San Remo was another favorite hangout for Village creative types. Opened in 1927, the bar occupied the first floor of a tenement building and was owned by mobsters. Tenements at best offered minimal-standard housing for impoverished families, and were present in many parts of New York City in the nineteenth and early twentieth centuries.

After World War II, the San Remo was one of the few bars open to a gay clientele, and it also welcomed beat writers. In his novel *The Subterraneans,* beat novelist Jack Kerouac described it as being "hip without being slick, intelligent without being corny," and its patrons as "intellectual as Hell without being pretentious or saying too much about it."*

In his novel he renamed the café the "Black Mask." Rumor has it that Kerouac met novelist Gore Vidal there and the two retired to the artsy Chelsea Hotel on 23rd Street for an intimate rendezvous. Socialist writer Michael Harrington described the café as a place where you might see "heterosexuals on the make; homosexuals who preferred erotic integration to the exclusively gay bars on Eighth Street; Communists; Socialists and Trotskyists; [and] potheads." Verifying Harrington's perception, Remo was celebrity-artist Andy Warhol's favorite place to pick up handsome young men whom he then employed at his Factory in the '60s and '70s. James Baldwin was another regular at the bar during his Village days. Authors William Burroughs and James Agee and jazz trumpet star Miles Davis were other attendees.**

Folk singer Fred Neil is pictured in front of the San Remo on the cover of his first album. Fred had hired Bob to play harmonica during his Café Wha? gigs. Fred was well known in the Village but was leading a double life. He was a contract songwriter, writing rock-and-roll songs for midtown music publisher Aaron Schroeder. One of these songs, "Candy Man," co-written with Beverly Ross, became a hit song in 1961 for Roy Orbison. Neil's Village folk fans had no idea that he was leading this secret musical life, and thought of him as a pure and commercially unsullied folksinger and singer-songwriter. Later Fred's song "Everybody's Talkin'" became a hit song in the movie *Midnight Cowboy,* performed by Harry Nilsson in 1969.

---

*Jack Kerouac, *The Subterraneans* (New York: Grove Press, 1958), 1.

**"San Remo Café," *Literary New York,* accessed June 6, 2022, www.literarymanhattan.org/place/san-remo-cafe/.

3. The cover of Fred Neil's first album, showing the singer in front of the San Remo Café.

The space is currently occupied by burger restaurant J.G. Melon, which has an outdoor dining space as well.

94, DYLAN'S TOWN HOUSE

Bob Dylan moved to Woodstock in 1963. He was intent on raising a family and wanted to escape into a less frantic environment than Manhattan offered. By 1970 the Dylan family received so many uninvited visitors that they decided to move back to the city. Consequently, Dylan purchased a townhouse in 1970 near his old Village haunts.

4. Dylan's townhouse on MacDougal Street.

Unfortunately, Dylan found that his celebrity status had removed any possibility of retaining his privacy. The principal offender was Alan Jules (A.J.) Weberman. Weberman created a career for himself as a "Dylanologist." In this role, Weberman assumed the role of Dylan's savior. His attitude was confrontational, akin to guerrilla theater. Weberman somehow found Dylan's home address and phone number and in addition to leading tours to the house, he would hold demonstrations where he and a small group of his cohorts shouted out that Dylan had sold out his ideals. He also made a habit of going through Bob's garbage, searching for clues about Dylan's personal habits and imaginary political skullduggery. He then turned this creepy approach into a pseudo-intellectual construct, by calling his exploits "garbology." Dylan fought back by peppering this garbage with used diapers, but such tactics backfired and seemed to stimulate Weberman rather than restrain him. Eventually he confronted Dylan on the street, and Dylan won a brief physical encounter.

5. Dylanologist A.J. Weberman conducting his research by dumpster diving in the Village. Photo: Chip Berlet. Creative Commons Share Alike 4.0 license.

A.J. then turned to a more intellectual approach, publishing books about Dylan that contained extensive and obscure explanations of Bob's lyrics and a manual that detailed garbology as a worthy scholarly endeavor. Weberman seemed to completely come off the rails in claiming that some of Dylan's songs were actually addressed to him. When Dylan was awarded the Nobel Prize in Literature in 2016, Weberman "modestly" claimed credit for bring Dylan to worldwide fame and attention through his own "scholarly" work.*

By 1973 Dylan had had enough, and he moved with his family to Southern California.

105, THE COMMONS COFFEEHOUSE

The Commons was a basket coffeehouse, opening in 1958. In basket houses, the performers were not paid by the management, but relied on the generosity of the customers, who placed tips for the performers in baskets passed around by the waitresses. I played several times at the Commons, and in fact the management *was* paying the performers. During the weekends that I worked, I recall the "pay" as being $3 a night. Passing the basket turned into a sort of sport for the waitresses. In traditional New York style, they became quite aggressive about ensuring that these contributions were being made, even to the point of taunting the less-generous customers,

During the time when I played at the Commons, beat poets John Brent and Hugh ("Wavy Gravy") Romney did poetry readings. The manager of the club was Luke Askew, who hailed from Northern Georgia, and his southern accent marked him as a kind of amiable Village redneck. Luke himself sometimes sang at the Gaslight, across the street from the Commons, and he also moonlighted as a furniture mover. He was friendly with the performers, and seemed to know every poet and musician in the Village. Later, he enjoyed a career as an actor in Hollywood, appearing in the films *Easy Rider*, *Cool Hand Luke*, and the spaghetti western *Night of the Serpent*.

Among the many others who graced its stage were Dominic Chianese, who later portrayed Uncle Junior in the TV series *The Sopranos*, who was on hand to sing operatic excerpts. An oddball singer specializing in the pop hits of the '30s,

---

*Robert Shelton, *No Direction Home: The Life and Music of Bob Dylan* (New York: Beech Tree Press, 1986), 420–423.

accompanying himself on ukulele, later became famous under the moniker Tiny Tim. Another eccentric performer, Agustin de Mello, was a flamenco guitarist. He was also a weight lifter and karate master, and when he felt irritated by an inattentive audience member, by his own personal demons, or by having his set cut short, de Mello would stand up and karate chop a board in half with his bare hands. That particular gesture certainly got everyone's attention. He briefly opened a venue at 175 Bleecker Street called the Dragon's Den.

6. Dominic Chianese at Folk City, 1966. Photo: Diana Jo Davies. Ralph Rinzler Folklife Archives and Collections, Diana Davies Collection, Smithsonian Center for Folklife and Cultural Heritage.

It was customary for guest performers to do short sets at the Commons to test new material or to amuse themselves. Among the guests that I saw were Paul (Noel) Stookey, in his pre–Peter, Paul and Mary days, performing what amounted to a standup comedy act. He would do imitations of car sounds, distinguished by the make and model of each vehicle. Toilet flushing sounds were also part of his repertoire of sounds.

WRITING "BLOWIN' IN THE WIND"

According to singer-songwriter David Blue (David Cohen), Dylan scribbled his first lyrics to his song "Blowin' in the Wind" while imbibing some caffeine at the Commons:

> I remember one afternoon [on April 16, 1962] we were sitting . . . drinking coffee, and Dylan started writing a song. He had his guitar and he was scribbling away, writing on a piece of paper. And he gave me his guitar and asked me to play various chords, while he worked on the words. When he finished it, we went over to Folk City and Bob played it for Gil Turner [a well-known social protest singer of the day], who thought it was fantastic. And then Gil got up on the stage and played it for the audience, while Bob stood in the shadows at the bar.*

The space was like a barn, poorly lit and larger than the nearby Gaslight. With a one-drink minimum, the owners encouraged a lot of turnover, to maximize profits. As Dave Van Ronk recalled, only half kidding, about the similar policy at the Gaslight, the owner "needed a way to clear out the current crowd after they had finished their cup of overpriced coffee, since no one would have bought a second cup of that slop. This presented a logistical problem to which the folk singers were the solution: you would get up and sing three songs, and if at the end of those three songs anybody was still left in the room, you were fired." The owners liked

---

*Allison Rapp, "60 Years Ago: Bob Dylan Debuts "Blowin' in the Wind," *UCR*, April 16, 2022, ultimateclassicrock.com/bob-dylan-blowin-in-the-wind/.

acts like Dylan, who could be relied upon to clear the house in the days when he was an unknown.*

From 1964 to 1968, the club was operated as the Café Feenjon, a sort of Near Eastern–Russian–Israeli music venue. The Feenjon moved to 40 West Eighth Street in 1989. After a 1968 remodel, the space was renamed the Fat Black Pussycat and expanded to be a 149-seat theater/café operated by Tom Ziegler (who also operated Café Figaro, down the street). A 1964 C-grade film named *The Fat Black Pussycat* after the club was promoted with a lurid description "a murdering maniac with a fetish for high heels [lurks in] New York's twilight world of beatniks and coffeehouses."**

Currently the location is used by Panchito's Mexican Restaurant. They took over the space in 1972, but the Pussycat name can still be seen, painted on the wall above Panchito's awning. An unrelated club at 130 West Third Street has taken the Pussycat name.

107, CAFÉ RIENZI

Café Rienzi was opened in the early 1950s by a group of partners, including visual artist David Grossblatt. Grossblatt had studied painting in Paris and then with Village artist-teacher Hans Hofmann. The coffeehouse was named after the hero of a nineteenth-century novel by English writer Edward Bulwer-Lytton. The book was later turned into an opera by Richard Wagner. Rienzi was a gathering place for artists, writers, musicians, and their friends.

108, THE DEN OF ANTIQUITY

A few doors down from the Folklore Center toward Bleecker Street on MacDougal Street was the colorful, dark, and dusty antique shop the Den of Antiquity. The store was owned by the husband-and-wife team of Shirley (Shani) Kaplan and Louis Young. Although the shop specialized in jewelry, anything was liable to turn up there. One night in 1958 I was walking out of the Folklore Center and saw Shani

---

*Dave Van Ronk with Elijah Wald, *The Mayor of MacDougal Street: A Memoir* (New York: Da Capo Press, 2005), 127–128.

**Daniel B. Schneider, "F.Y.I.," *New York Times*, May 16, 1999, www.nytimes.com/1999/05/16/nyregion/fyi-693685.html.

walking down the street carrying a banjo in a hard case. After a brief dialogue with her, I bought the banjo, an old Vega Tubaphone Special Deluxe Five String Banjo, for $110. This was the highest-level Tubaphone model. The line included nine numerically graded banjos, a Special Model, and the capstone of the line, the Special Deluxe. In today's dollars, this banjo is worth somewhere between $15,000 and $25,000. Finding such a banjo might well prove more difficult than affording it! It was, by the way, in perfect condition, ready to play. Why did I ever sell it?

The Den was closed in 2007 when Kaplan died. It is currently home to a dry cleaner and a custom clothing store.

110, THE FOLKLORE CENTER

7. Izzy Young in the Folklore Center, early 1960s. Photo: Diana Jo Davies. Ralph Rinzler Folklife Archives and Collections, Diana Davies Collection, Smithsonian Center for Folklife and Cultural Heritage.

By the time Bob Dylan got to New York City, folk dancer, book dealer, and small-scale entrepreneur Israel Goodman Young had established the Folklore Center, the center of all things folk in the Village. The store opened in 1957 and sold a handful of banjos, guitars, and mandolins, many books about folk music, some records and music instruction books, and various regional and national magazines that featured articles about folk music and folk singers. Village musicians made sure that Izzy, as everyone called him, had their newest records for sale.

Izzy was a force of nature in the folk music revival. He wrote a sort of combination of facts and gossip column called "Frets and Frails" for the folk music magazine *Sing Out!* He would occasionally close the store and lead Morris or square dances on the streets of the Village. Touring musicians used the store as a mail drop; there were frequent jam sessions and Izzy would even allow musicians to occasionally sleep at the store.

None of this adequately explains Izzy's personality. On several occasions I witnessed Izzy throw people out of the store for some violation of his personal ethical code. It got to be a badge of honor for musicians to claim that they had been thrown out of the Folklore Center at one time or another. On a more endearing level, I also was present on several occasions when the store was filled with people and Izzy decided that he needed to grab something to eat at a nearby café. He would simply ask a customer, often someone he had never seen before, to "watch the store, while I grab a sandwich." Never mind that there were thousand-dollar guitars hanging on the walls! To the best of my knowledge, this never resulted in any thefts or untoward acts. Oddly enough, some forty years later I witnessed Rick Kelly, owner of Carmine Street Guitars, do exactly the same thing. In both instances I was truly astonished that in a massive city like New York, a store owner would exhibit such trust in anonymous customers.

The Folklore Center was like a magnet, drawing musicians, writers, and folk music fans into its orbit. One of Izzy's good friends was Jack Prelutsky. Jack was both a musician and a writer, and he sang in clubs under the name Jack Ballard, as well as giving guitar lessons. Later Jack became an award-winning author of numerous children's books. A casual trip to the Folklore Center might include encounters with famous and little-known musicians, agents and managers looking for fresh talent to exploit, and even representatives of successful commercial folk singers looking to buy books that might contain new material for their clients to perform at shows. When jam sessions spontaneously erupted, Izzy would often lock the doors to keep gawkers and tourists out. No one accused Izzy of being a brilliant businessman, and he often was barely able to pay his bills. You could always count on him to express an opinion about artists or music business practices. The general consensus was that he might have been an opinionated curmudgeon, but he was generally honest and forthright and uninterested in personal gain.

By 1965 rents on MacDougal Street had skyrocketed, so Izzy moved his store to 321 Sixth Avenue. In 1973 he moved to Stockholm, and opened the Folklore Centrum there. A dry cleaner and a custom clothing store currently occupy the old Folklore Center.

IZZY AND BOB DYLAN

8. Izzy Young photographed through the window of the Folklore Center. Photo: Sound Associates. From the Ronald D. Cohen Collection #20239, Southern Folklife Collection, The Wilson Library, University of North Carolina at Chapel Hill.

Izzy Young was one of the first entrepreneurs in New York to recognize Bob Dylan's talent. In Izzy's regular column in folk music magazine *Sing Out!* he frequently commented on Dylan's activities. In return, Dylan wrote "Talkin' Folklore Center," a song that was a tribute to the Folklore Center based on Woody Guthrie's various talking blues songs. In the song, Dylan actually recommends that people go down to the Folklore Center and buy records or books. Here are a few excerpts from the song:

> You get a bumper, and I'll get a fender,
> We'll go down to the Folklore Center.
> You get a daft and I'll get dizzy,
> We'll go down to see old Izzy.
> What did the button say to the suspender?
> You've got to support the Folklore Center.[*]

Eat your heart out, Woody Guthrie!

In November, 1961, Izzy presented Dylan in his first solo concert. The performance took place in Carnegie Chapter Hall, a smaller hall on the fifth floor of the more famous Carnegie Hall. The room could hold 200 people, but the attendance was only 53. This event was significant because it marked the beginnings of Dylan's career as a concert artist, as opposed to a coffeehouse or barroom singer. Fifty years later, Dylan continues to perform internationally as a concert artist.

113, MINETTA TAVERN

The Minetta Tavern opened in 1937. Originally a speakeasy called the Black Rabbit, it took its name from Minetta Brook, which once ran from 23rd street, meandering south and west until it reached the Hudson River on the west side. The tavern featured cheap bar fare, attracting artists and writers. A 2009 renovation turned the place into an upscale French restaurant.

In its heyday many writers, including E.E. Cummings and Joe Gould (a.k.a. "Professor Seagull"), hung out here. The poet Cummings lived at nearby Patchin Place for some forty years. Novelist Djuna Barnes lived in a nearby building. Cummings was fond of beginning his day by opening his window and yelling "Djuna, are you still alive?" Joe Gould was a true Village character and the alleged author of an enormous

---

*See "Talking Folklore Center" at *Bob Dylan's Musical Roots*, accessed Jun 6, 2022, www. bobdylanroots.com/folklore.html; see also Aaron Galbraith and Tony Attwood, "'Talkin' Folklore Center' Bob Dylan's Early Talking Blues," *Untold Dylan*, June 8, 2019, bob-dylan. org.uk/archives/10512.

manuscript called *The Oral History of the World*. Joe was a 1911 graduate of Harvard University. He would read aloud while panhandling the bar, as well as any other place where he wandered. As the in-residence pre-hippie, Gould was allowed a free meal a day, but it had to be one of the lowest-priced items on the menu! Most of the time he lived on ketchup and sugar packages. He created a language of his own that he called Sea Gull, claiming that he had learned how to speak this bird language. Part of his act at the tavern was to read famous poems translated into this language, which led to him becoming known as Professor Sea Gull. Gould is memorialized in the bar in an oil painting that is part of a wall display of Village caricatures.

No actual Gould manuscript has ever been found, although Joe always carried folders with him that supposedly were related to his master work. He was able to convince various apartment managers that his work would be published imminently. He pulled this routine repeatedly, going from room to room without having to pay rent. To help convince his landladies, he would leave pages of the alleged manuscript with them. Many scholars believe that in fact it never existed. However, the indefatigable Israel Young turned up manuscript files after Joe died. According to Greenwich Village historian Terry Miller, these files are basically transcriptions of conversations that Gould heard in his Village meanderings. Gould's diaries do survive, and are now housed at NYU. The notion of this eccentric's dairies being preserved at an expensive private university would likely have amused old Joe. Gould died in 1955, but Joseph Mitchell's book *Joe Gould's Secret* deconstructed the legend in 1964.

114, THE KETTLE OF FISH

The Kettle of Fish was a bar that was located above the next-door Gaslight Café. It opened in 1950, and some ten years later Dylan hung out there. Performers often would get a drink there before or after performing sets at the Gaslight. There was also a long-standing poker game that was frequented by Bob Dylan, songwriter Tom Paxton, Dave Van Ronk, and Dylan's other friends and associates. Blues scholar and booking agent Dick Waterman recalled that it "had a bar on the left and a middle aisle all the way back to the restrooms. . . . Bob Dylan and his manager, Albert Grossman, always sat at the back table with their backs against the air conditioner, looking at the room."* Tom Paxton adds, "It was really the Kettle of Fish where all

---

*Robbie Woliver, *Hoot! A 25-Year History of the Greenwich Village Folk Scene* (New York: St. Martin's Press, 1994).

the ideas, gossip, songs and friendships were exchanged."* Folk singer Pat Foster was known to drink to excess here, and eventually was banned for unruly behavior. Shortly thereafter, Pat appeared on a local TV show hosted by legendary disc jockey Art Ford. The bartender had the TV on, and was nonplussed to see his former patron featured on the popular show.

The original bar moved twice and is now located in the West Village off Sheridan Square on Christopher Street. The current occupant of the original site is the Saigon Shack.

DAVE VAN RONK

Dave Van Ronk was a key influence on Bob Dylan's music and his knowledge of politics and the arts. Along with his wife Terri Thal, he was active in left-wing politics, especially the anti-Stalin Trotskyite factions in New York. Van Ronk was a fairly well-established folk singer and knew everything there was to know about Greenwich Village venues. Thal had begun to manage Dave, and took on managing Dylan as a sort of favor. When Al Grossman became interested in managing Bob, she cheerfully withdrew from any business affiliation with Dylan.

9. Dave and Terri Van Ronk, ca. 1960. Photo: Sound Associates. From the Ronald D. Cohen Collection #20239, Southern Folklife Collection, The Wilson Library, University of North Carolina at Chapel Hill.

---

*Tammy L. Turner, *Dick Waterman: A Life in Blues* (Jackson: University Press of Mississippi, 2019), chapter 2.

I have never seen any evidence that Dylan was especially interested in politics in his Minnesota days. It seems reasonable to conclude that Bob's contact with the Van Ronks and his then-girlfriend Suze Rotolo's family—together with the positive reception of his early finger-pointing songs—introduced him into the world of politics and social protest music. Dave and Bob had a friendly and kind of joking relationship that accompanied their poker games, drinking, and coffee klatches. At one point, Dave bet Bob that he couldn't write a song that used the hook "If I had to do it all over again, Babe, I'd do it all over you"; Dylan quickly wrote the song, and Dave recorded it on a 1963 album.

10. Dave Van Ronk onstage, ca. 1963. Photo: Sound Associates. From the Ronald D. Cohen Collection #20239, Southern Folklife Collection, The Wilson Library, University of North Carolina at Chapel Hill.

A famous feud between the two performers occurred when Dave Van Ronk was working on a solo album while Dylan was recording his 1964 debut LP for Columbia Records. Dave had worked out an arrangement of the rarely collected folk song "The House of the Rising Sun." Dylan liked the song and the arrangement and started performing it himself. When Dave got ready to record, he asked Bob not to record this song. The trouble was that Dylan had already recorded the song. This caused a rift between the two that eventually healed, but not entirely so. Two years later the British rock band The Animals had a huge hit record that basically used Van Ronk's adaptation of the song.*

116, THE GASLIGHT CAFÉ

11. Gaslight Café building.

---

*See Suze Rotolo, *A Freewheelin' Time: A Memoir of Greenwich Village in the Sixties* (New York: Broadway Books, 2007), and Shelton, *No Direction Home*.

The Gaslight Café and Gerde's Folk City were the two most important clubs in the Village for folk music performers and fans in Dylan's day. The club was located below the Kettle of Fish in what was the building's basement. The club was opened in 1958 as a basket house by John Mitchell. Mitchell had driven to New York from Pittsburgh, and supposedly discovered the club when his car got a flat tire on MacDougal Street.

Before John Mitchell opened the Gaslight, he had previously operated the Café Figaro at the corner of MacDougal and Bleecker Streets. Village raconteur/ author Al Aronowitz remembers Mitchell as "a master carpenter, a star con man, a resourceful innovator, a proud individualist and a cagey entrepreneur who helped establish the coffee house as a Greenwich Village countercultural institution." When Mitchell first saw the basement location, he realized that the ceiling was too low to accommodate an audience. Undeterred, in Aronowitz's words, he "couldn't raise the ceiling so he lowered the floor. It was all dirt, and he shoveled it out by hand. Except, the city refused him a building permit and so he had to load the dirt in sacks and get rid of it as if he were tunneling his way out of prison. At night, he would carry the sacks out onto MacDougal Street and dump a little dirt into each of the garbage pails on the block."* Mitchell reportedly was unwilling to pay off the cops, which may have led to his frequent citations for violations of various city codes or regulations.

Mitchell waged constant battles with city inspectors and alleged Mafia figures who wanted the club closed. One of the controversies involved the wrath of the tenants of the building, who were irritated by the applause coming from the club. This resulted in noise complaints to the police. To cut back on the noise, Mitchell insisted that the audience show its appreciation by snapping their fingers rather than clapping their hands. This custom became part of the hip lexicon, spreading far afield. Dylan himself lived briefly in one of the apartments, as did Dave Van Ronk. Although Mitchell was no Peter Pan, from time to time he would allow indigent performers to sleep in the club.

Originally the club's performers were primarily "beat poets," including Allen Ginsberg, Hugh Romney, and Gregory Corso, novelist Jack Kerouac, and comedian Bill Cosby. Len Chandler was the first musical act, although he too started out as a

---

*Al Aronowitz, "How Do You Bury a Cellar?" *The Blacklisted Journalist*, February 1, 1996, www.blacklistedjournalist.com/column6b.html.

12. Gaslight Café basement stairs entrance.

performing poet. Cosby made quite a splash here, and scores of folk singers, known and unknown, debuted here and went on to record and tour nationally. In Dylan's earliest years in the Village, he was not regarded as a major talent, but just another struggling folk singer. At one of Bob's early appearances on a hootenanny night (a sort of musical open-mike night where performers took turns singing and playing), poet Hugh Romney introduced Dylan as "A legend in his life time . . . Uh . . . What's your name kid?"*

*Kasper van Laarhoven, "The Story of the Gaslight Café, Where Dylan Premiered 'A Hard Rain's a-Gonna Fall,'" *Bedford + Bowery*, December 28, 2016, bedfordandbowery.com/2016/12/the-story-of-the-gaslight-cafe-where-dylan-premiered-a-hard-rains-a-gonna-fall/.

In his memoir, *Chronicles,* Dylan emphasized the importance of the club to him. "I kept my eyes on the Gaslight. How could I not? Compared to it, the rest of the places on the street were nameless and miserable, low-level basket houses or small coffee houses where the performer passed the hat."* In 2005, Dylan allowed Columbia Records to release an "official bootleg" titled *Live at the Gaslight 1962.* It consisted of three original songs and seven traditional ones, reflecting Dylan's performances before he became fully committed to a career as a singer-songwriter. Dylan reports being paid $60 a week at the Gaslight.

Anyone who ordered food at the Gaslight Café was risking a visit to the Emergency Room. The waiters were all beatniks who were there to enjoy the scene, and they paid scant attention to the customers. Dave Van Ronk captured the topsy-turvy scene in the second verse of his song, "Gaslight Rag":

> I had a dream that the Gaslight was clean,
> And rats were all scrubbed down.
> The coffee was great and the waitresses straight,
> And Patrick Sky left town.
> No one was swocked and Dylan played Bach,
> And Ochs' songs all scanned.
> I got out of bed and I straightened my head,
> And started a rock-n-roll band.

The song concluded, "There's not much light, but there's plenty of fights when you're singing in a hole in the ground."**

Mitchell sold the club in 1961 and the new owners, the Hood family, brought in mostly folk music performers. Among the noteworthy performers were Dylan's mentor Dave Van Ronk, singer-songwriters Joni Mitchell (with her then-husband Chuck in their New York debut in 1966) and Phil Ochs, Richie Havens (of later Woodstock fame), traditional bluesmen Jesse Fuller and Mississippi John Hurt, and many others. The rock-blues group The Blues Project supposedly did their first public performance at the club in late 1965. Toward the end of the '60s the club was managed by folksinger Gil Robbins, father of actor Tim Robbins.

---

*Bob Dylan, *Chronicles: Volume One* (New York: Simon & Schuster, 2004), 151–152.
**Van Ronk with Wald, *The Mayor of MacDougal Street,* 151–152.

In 1969 I was producing records for a subsidiary of ABC Records, and attended a music showcase for Loudon Wainwright III at the Gaslight. Wainwright had been receiving many write-ups in the music business periodical *Record World*. In this small and rather dinky club I noticed executives from Atlantic and Liberty records in attendance, along with Loudon's manager and a group of young women who had apparently been recruited by Loudon's manager to wildly applaud after each song. Incidentally, Atlantic Records did sign Wainwright to a contract. In the early '70s performers like Odetta, David Bromberg, and jazz composer and bassist Charles Mingus played here. The original club closed in 1967, reopened a year later, and finally shuttered in 1971.

In 2013, the Coen Brothers made a film called *Inside Llewyn Davis,* very loosely based on the life and career of Dave Van Ronk. They recreated the Gaslight's façade for the movie. The Amazon TV series *The Marvelous Miss Maisel* similarly attempted to recreate the Gaslight as the venue where the fictional lead character got her start in standup comedy. Insomnia Cookies and Ink Body and Art currently occupy the premises.

116, CARICATURE UPSTAIRS

Caricature was a small coffee shop located above the Gaslight. This venue was tiny, but had two rooms. One of them often hosted a bridge games that included Liz, the proprietor. In the smaller back room, musicians were allowed to sing and play, but only if they did not disturb the bridge game. Dave Van Ronk and Bob Dylan often had coffee there, and Van Ronk mentioned in his memoir *The Mayor of Mac-Dougal Street* that he could always count on Liz to provide hamburgers, whether or not he had the cash to actually pay for them. Like Izzy Young at the Folklore Center, she would occasionally lose patience with musicians and throw them out of the place. I found numerous musicians who remembered Liz, but not one of them could recall her last name.

DYLAN'S PEERS AT THE GASLIGHT

Bob Dylan often hung out at the Gaslight, the performers' room upstairs, or the adjacent Kettle of Fish bar. Bob would often do guest sets late in the evening, even though he was not on the bill. With many of his friends in attendance, it was a good place for him to try out new songs. There was a regular group of poker players, friends, and drinkers who all socialized with one another. None of these musicians became as famous as Bob, but several went on to successful recording and/or songwriting careers.

When he showed up at the Gaslight, Tom Paxton was just getting out of the service and still sported an army haircut, which made other performers and poets suspicious that he was a narcotics cop. Tom went on to write many political songs, but his most commercially successful songs, recorded by numerous artists, included "Rambling Boy," "I Can't Help But Wonder Where I'm Bound," and his unlikely rock hit song, "Bottle of Wine."

13. Len Chandler performing at the Broadside apartment, 1967. Photo: Diana Jo Davies. Ralph Rinzler Folklife Archives and Collections, Diana Davies Collection, Smithsonian Center for Folklife and Cultural Heritage.

Len Chandler was one of the few black singer-songwriters on the '60s folk scene. Len was an activist in the civil rights movement, and served numerous stints in southern jail for his efforts. His song "Beans in My Ear," recorded in 1964 by the Serendipity Singers, was well on the way to becoming a hit song until ear, nose, and throat doctors found that kids were following the song's instructions! The doctors successfully lobbied to have the song removed from radio. Len was classically trained, with a master's degree in oboe performance. This level of musical training was a rarity among folk music performers. Another black performer was Hal Waters. Waters was one of Bob's poker-playing friends and was a smooth-voiced cabaret singer.

Paul Clayton was a trained folklorist who made dozens of recordings singing songs of various occupations or localities. When Dylan began to write songs, he often used traditional tunes with new and colorful lyrics. Dylan learned his songs from recordings, but Clayton had done a considerable amount of folk song collecting. He rearranged one of these songs as "Who's Gonna Buy You Ribbons (When I'm Gone)?" Bob used that exact tune for his hit song "Don't Think Twice, It's All Right." This ended up in a lawsuit between Paul and Bob's publishers, but it didn't seem to jeopardize their friendship. Clayton went on several automobile trips-tours with Dylan. Clayton's career was cut short by various drug and personal problems, and he committed suicide in 1967.

14. Phil Ochs performing at the Philadelphia Folk Festival, 1968. Photo: Diana Jo Davies. Ralph Rinzler Folklife Archives and Collections, Diana Davies Collection, Smithsonian Center for Folklife and Cultural Heritage.

Singer-songwriter Phil Ochs had a sort of friendly rivalry with Bob Dylan. Although Bob turned away from writing heavily political songs in the mid-'60s, Ochs continued to write such songs throughout his career. Ochs admired and respected Dylan, but Dylan did not always reciprocate these feelings. In one famous incident, Bob threw Ochs out of a limousine when Phil criticized a particular line of one of Dylan's songs. Dylan then shouted that Ochs was a journalist, not a songwriter.* Like Clayton, Ochs committed suicide in 1976, sometime after being diagnosed with bipolar disorder. Several of his songs, including "The Power and the Glory," "I Ain't Marching Anymore," and "There but for Fortune" have been recorded by various artists, including Joan Baez.

115, CAFÉ WHA?

15. Café Wha?

---

*Heylin, *The Double Life of Bob Dylan*, 385–386.

When Dylan came to new the Village in 1961, he immediately was able to snag a gig, sort of, at Café Wha?, another one of the one of the many basket houses in the Village. It was owned by the late Manny Roth, who was the uncle of hard rock vocalist David Lee Roth. Manny was later celebrated as the Duke of MacDougal Street, and the café still exists today. As Roth's *New York Times* obituary stated:

> In 1959 someone told Mr. Roth about a garage that used to be an old horse stable on MacDougal, between Bleecker and West Third Streets. You had to go down steep stairs to reach the dark, dank basement which was bisected by a trough once used as a gutter for horse dung. Mr. Roth immediately recognized it as an excellent site for a coffee house. He spent his last $100 on a truckload of broken marble to make the floor, which he personally laid. He sprayed the walls with black paint to create the feeling of a cave. There were castoff chairs and candles in blue glass flickering on every table. Full occupancy was 325.*

On his arrival in New York on Monday, January 24, 1961, Dylan came to the club. The obituary recounts that he approached Roth and said, "Just got here from the West. Name's Bob Dylan. I'd like to do a few songs? Can I?" It happened that Monday was hootenanny night, when anyone could perform, so Roth invited him to the stage, where Dylan sang two songs by his idol Woody Guthrie.**

Roth even asked the audience to help find Dylan a place where he could crash, so Dylan spent his first night in New York City rent free. The Wha was unusual among Village coffeehouses because it featured entertainment in the afternoon as well as in the evening. Following his open-mike performance, Bob in effect joined the B team, playing solo during the afternoons. His "pay" was $1 a day plus a hamburger.

The better-drawing performers played in the evenings, and steel drum player Victor "Superman" Brady was the star and primary draw at the club. In the evenings, Bob also played harmonica behind Fred Neil. Karen Dalton, whom Dylan termed "the best folksinger in the Village," was Neil's friend, and often performed with him at the Wha. The first known photo of Dylan performing in the Village shows him

---

*Douglas Martin, "Manny Roth, 94, Impresario of Cafe Wha?, Is Dead," *New York Times*, August 1, 2014.

**Shelton, *No Direction Home*, 94.

playing harmonica with Neil and Dalton. Although Karen was virtually unknown during her lifetime, in the last two years she has been the subject of two lengthy documentary films. Although she only recorded two albums during her lifetime, a half dozen other albums have emerged since her death in 1993, and her friend Peter Walker put together an album of her lyrics set to music by various artists, including Lucinda Williams.

Roth was known to be notoriously tightfisted—in fact, Dave Van Ronk said that "by the time (Roth) got finished with a penny, you could no longer see the Lincoln on it." Dylan wrote that "he wore a tomato-stained apron . . . [and] had a fleshy, hard-bitten face, bulging cheeks, scars on his face like the marks of claws—thought of himself as a lady's man—saving his money so he could go to Verona in Italy to visit the tomb of Romeo and Juliet." Dylan was fired by Roth after he failed to turn up for several scheduled shows.*

Among the other performers at the Wha were Paul (Noel) Stookey, who was one of the founders of the hit group Peter, Paul and Mary. Mary Travers was briefly a waitress at the Wha before she became a successful singer. Actor-to-be Louis Gossett Jr. started out as a Greenwich Village folksinger, and in 1966 fabled rock guitarist Jimi Hendrix had a three-month engagement at the Wha, using the name Jimmy James and the Blue Flames. In 1967 a New Jersey bar band, The Castiles, played the room. They featured a young musician named Bruce Springsteen.

Roth closed the club in 1968 but it was reopened in the '70s under new ownership. The Players Theatre now shares the location with a revived Café Wha?

119, CAFFE REGGIO

A few doors down from the Wha is the Caffe Reggio. Reggio imported the first Italian espresso machine to the Village in 1927. The café was opened by Italian immigrant and barber Domenico Parisi. The giant espresso machine was described in a 1955 *New Yorker* spot as "one of the biggest and most frightening urns in the Village. Frightening because in drawing a *cappucino*, [Parisi] releases a valve which . . . emit[s] an appalling, ripping sound, like a barrage of rockets fired from a dive bomber. . . . [The noise] fills you with a sudden, insane desire to leap to

---

*Martin, "Manny Roth, 94, Impresario of Cafe Wha?, Is Dead."

your feet, blunder through the door and run all the way across town for a plunge in the East River."*

16. Domenico Parisi working the espresso machine at the Caffe Reggio. Library of Congress, Prints and Photographs Division.

This coffeehouse was a homey and inviting respite for locals and for the many tourists who flocked to the Village in search of entertainment. The well-heated interior made it a favorite winter-time hangout for neighborhood regulars and tourists, but few folk singers or beatniks. I spent many an hour there warming myself and

---

*A clipping of the article is reproduced on the website of Caffe Reggio, at www.caffereggio.com/press/; the exact issue and page of the original piece may be discovered by someone who has access to a collection of *The New Yorker* dating to 1955.

devoured their delicious Italian pastry cannoli, but cannot recall ever encountering any folk singers or singer-songwriters there.

The Reggio has been immortalized in films ranging from *The Godfather Part II* to *Next Stop, Greenwich Village* to *Inside Llewyn Davis*. Another part of its storied history is that John F. Kennedy made his first presidential campaign stop here. The Caffe Reggio is still open and has been operating with an outdoor eating area added since the coronavirus struck. It is one of the last unsullied remnants of Dylan's 1961-era Greenwich Village.

VILLAGE ATTITUDE

Vince Martin was a likable and capable singer who had one hit record, "Cindy, Oh Cindy." The song was a rewrite of an old folk song called "Pay Me My Money Down." The authors were Robert Nemiroff, playwright Lorraine Hansberry's husband, and Burt D'Lugoff, brother of Village Gate owner Art D'Lugoff.

One day in the late '50s I was walking down MacDougal Street and ran into Vince with his accompanist, the excellent banjoist and guitarist Billy Faier. I knew that they had been playing out of town, and asked what they were doing in the Village on a Friday night. Billy told me that the duo had a booking at a college, and being carefree folksingers, didn't read the contract too closely. They remembered something about Lawrence College, so at around 6 p.m. they drove up to all-women's college Sarah Lawrence College, north of New York City in Bronxville, New York. They spotted a building that seemed to be hosting a social function. Vince explained to the hostess that they were there to do a concert. The hostess looked puzzled, and explained that the only thing going on was a dance. Vince took out the contract, and realized that the gig was at St. Lawrence University, which is located 377 miles north of New York City. That's why I saw them on MacDougal Street—in typical folkie fashion, they just didn't pay that much attention to the business end of their careers. As the saying goes, I guess they didn't make the gig. It undoubtedly would have been entertaining to listen to Vince explaining to his agent why they never made it!

133, PROVINCETOWN PLAYHOUSE

17. Provincetown Playhouse, ca. 1920. New York Public Library Digital Collections.

This historic theater was named for the Provincetown Players. Its original location, dating to 1916, was a few doors away at 139. It moved to 133 two years later. The original company included Eugene O'Neill, Edna St. Vincent Millay, and Djuna Barnes. African American singer and actor Paul Robeson performed here, and the theater produced E.E. Cummings's play *Him*. Future movie stars Bette Davis and Claudette Colbert made their New York stage debut at this theater.

The building, which was originally a stable and a wine-bottling plant, was acquired by New York University, and is now used by the NYU Theater Department.

NYU is a massive presence in the Village and, as is the case with a number of large urban universities, has had some conflicts with neighborhood preservationists, who are resistant to modernization of historic facilities.

CORNER EIGHTH STREET AND MACDOUGAL STREET, EIGHTH STREET BOOKSHOP

The original bookstore was founded by brothers Elias (Eli) and Ted Wilentz. The three-story shop attracted everyone from the beats to older poets like W.H. Auden. The bookshop was a departure from the most of the Village's grittier hangouts, because it was clean, well lit, and well organized. You could browse at length without being hassled by the management. Employees were always polite, well dressed, and friendly to the customers. In 1959 the brothers expanded the business to found Corinth Books, an early publisher of the beats and titles of local interest.

Ted Wilentz's wife Joan described the store as "being the equivalent of a singles bar in the '50s. It was such an exciting venue. We just drooled over the titles available. There was just a wave of exciting talents in that post–World War II generation that partied at each other's houses."* Village poet, provocateur, sometime owner of his own bookstore, and leader of the band The Fugs, Ed Sanders recalled that "The Eighth Street Bookshop was pivotal to a young poet in those days. It was there that I monitored little magazines . . . and where I first purchased Allen Ginsberg's epochal *Kaddish and Other Poems*."** Bob Dylan first met Allen Ginsberg at this store at a party in 1964.

In 1965, the bookstore moved to a larger location across the street at 17 West Eighth Street. In 1976, fire almost destroyed the store, and although it was rebuilt, it never fully recovered, closing in 1979. Critic Sean Wilentz is Eli's nephew; he is a professor at Princeton University, and he has written numerous books about American history, as well as the book *Bob Dylan in America*. The first floor of the original building is now occupied by Oregon coffee purveyors Stumptown Coffee Roasters.

---

*Kevin Howell, "Consummate Bookseller Ted Wilentz Dies at 86," *Publishers Weekly*, May 17, 2001, www.publishersweekly.com/pw/print/20010514/37928-consummate-bookseller-ted-wilentz-dies-at-86.html.

**Kembrew McLeod, *The Downtown Pop Underground: New York City and the Literary Punks, Renegade Artists, DIY Filmmakers, Mad Playwrights, and Rock 'n' Roll Glitter Queens Who Revolutionized Culture* (New York: Abrams Press, 2018).

3

Bleecker Street

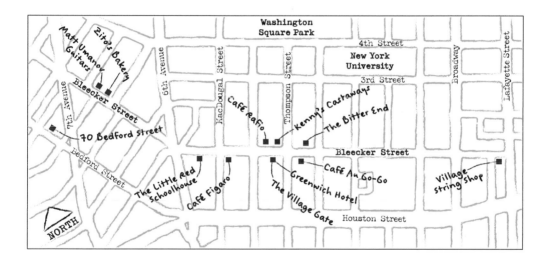

Bleecker Street runs east and west, connecting the Bowery and the East Village to Abingdon Square. Just as Houston Street could have been named Zero Street, Bleecker substitutes for First Street. MacDougal Street had kind of a bargain basement feel; the basket coffeehouses were relatively cheap, and even the Gaslight wasn't paying top dollar to major league acts. Bleecker Street had a more expansive feel, and the entertainment clubs were larger venues, featured bigger acts, paid them better, and charged more money to customers.

56, VILLAGE STRING SHOP

Luthier Peter Carbone held forth at his tiny shop in the Village. Carbone's shop was one of the few places where a musician could buy silk-and-steel guitar strings.

These strings were a sort of compromise between nylon and steel strings, producing a sound between the two. Many of the first generation of revival folksingers would hang out at the store to visit the soft-spoken Carbone. Pete Seeger was a customer, and so was Erik Darling. Although Darling is not well known to the current generation of folksingers, he was a member of the band The Tarriers, who had one of the first folk-pop hits, "Day-O (The Banana Boat Song)," in 1956. During the "folk scare" of the '60s, Erik founded the Rooftop Singers, who had a gigantic hit in 1963 with the old jug band song "Walk Right In." That song featured two twelve-string guitars, thereby sparking a revival of interest in that instrument. Later, at Pete Seeger's suggestion, Erik replaced him in the Weavers when Pete left to pursue a solo career. Erik also recorded several important and under-rated solo albums.

147, THE BITTER END

This venue started out in life in the late 1950s as a coffee house known as the Cock and Bull, and poets and comedians performed there. In 1961 Fred Weintraub bought the club and renamed it. Weintraub had already led a colorful life, playing piano in a bordello, operating a fishing boat in Cuba, and roaming around Europe. Over the next decades, he introduced relatively unknown talent at the club, including such artists as comedians Lenny Bruce and Billy Crystal and singers Randy Newman, Joni Mitchell, and Peter, Paul and Mary. Like the fabled hungry i nightclub in San Francisco, the Bitter End had distinctive brick walls, which set it apart from other Village venues.

In 1965 Weintraub hired Paul Colby to manage the club, but when Colby opened a bar next door known as the Other End, Weintraub fired him. Colby directly competed with Weintraub by featuring folk artists at his club. Nevertheless, in 1974 Weintraub sold the Bitter End to him. The club only held 150 people with standing room for 80 more. It built a reputation as a good listening room and, despite its size, Colby was able to book such major acts as Stevie Wonder, Jackson Browne, and Neil Diamond who generally played larger and more lucrative venues.

Like Weintraub, Colby had a varied background. He worked as a shipping clerk, had a job delivering sheet music for a music publisher, and then became a music promoter, running personal errands for Frank Sinatra in Los Angeles. When he returned to New York he became a furniture maker, selling his creations to various music business stars. Colby reserved a booth for Bob Dylan at the club so that he could be seated with a minimum of fuss. The club remains open today.

152, CAFÉ AU GO GO

Howard and Elly Solomon operated the Café Au Go Go from 1964 to 1969. The club originally featured jazz and comedy acts, like pianist Bill Evans, saxophone Player Stan Getz, and comedians George Carlin and Lenny Bruce. Bruce was arrested at the club along with Solomon while performing his act, and was charged with various obscenity violations. The club later became an important Village music venue, focusing on rock acts with occasional blues or folk singers. Among the acts who appeared there were the Grateful Dead, Richie Havens, Van Morrison, Judy Collins, The Doors, and The Yardbirds. Solomon sold the club to Richie Havens and a partner in 1969, but it closed soon after.

Solomon also created and managed the Café Au Go Go Singers, a large pop-folk group modeled after the New Christy Minstrels. Two of the musicians in that group were Richie Furay and Stephen Stills, who were later bandmates in Buffalo Springfield. Furay left that group to form Poco, while Stills became a rock superstar in the band Crosby, Stills, and Nash.

157, KENNY'S CASTAWAYS

From 1976 to 2012, this club boasted the sign "Through these portals walk the famous." Kenny's began its life as a bar, evolving into an uptown East Side club. In an earlier location, it featured the glam band the New York Dolls. When the lease ran out, owner Pat Kenny moved the club to Bleecker Street. He was attracted to local, little-known musicians, whom he termed "castaways." Bruce Springsteen played some of his first shows at Kenny's, and other artists who performed there included Yoko Ono, Patti Smith, the Fugees, and blues composer Willie Dixon. The music at Kenny's covered a wide range including jazz, rock, hip-hop, blues, and folk.

The building itself was a gay bar in the early 1890s, and it made no attempt to disguise its attitude or preferences. After the 2012 closing of the club it began a new life as Carroll's Place, an "Italian-American wine bar and gastropub."

158–160, GREENWICH HOTEL AND THE VILLAGE GATE

The Greenwich Hotel was originally a workingmen's residence, one of three model buildings built by millionaire philanthropist Darius Ogden Mills. Mills died in 1910, and the property deteriorated into a flophouse. The building briefly was home to the coffeehouse Jazz on the Wagon.

In 1958 entrepreneur Art D'Lugoff turned the basement of the property into a thriving jazz club called the Village Gate, and later added a piano bar called Top of the Gate. The club was best known as a jazz venue, featuring a stylistically varied music menu that included such greats as Miles Davis, John Coltrane, Bill Evans, and Thelonious Monk. D'Lugoff had eclectic tastes and he also featured B.B. King, Aretha Franklin, Pete Seeger, Jimi Hendrix, harmonica virtuoso Larry Adler, singer-pianist Nina Simone, and comics Richard Pryor and Mort Sahl. There were even occasional classical music shows, one of which featured a premiere of a piece by longtime Village resident and electronic music pioneer Edgard Varèse. There was also a series that paired well-known jazz musicians with Latin artists.

Always searching for new entertainment, the club also presented some significant off-Broadway theater. These shows included the critically acclaimed *Jacques Brel Is Alive and Well and Living in Paris*, *MacBird!*—a Vietnam-era political satire—and a musical about black vaudeville titled *One Mo' Time*. In 1974 he presented a musical at the club called *Let My People Come*. Because the show was presented by male and female performers who were almost all naked, the State Liquor Authority tried to close the close and lifted the club's liquor license. D'Lugoff won the court case and the show ran for two and a half years.

Like his fellow Bleecker Street club owners, D'Lugoff himself had a rich and complicated career. He was an encyclopedia salesman, a waiter at the Catskill Mountains borscht-belt hotels, a cab driver in Los Angeles, a tree surgeon's assistant in upstate New York, and a union organizer in Massachusetts and Kentucky. Over the years the club expanded to three performance venues, but by 1994 it became the victim of rising rents and changing music tastes. It briefly opened midtown on West 52nd Street in 1996, but did not last out the year. D'Lugoff died in 2008.

One night in the mid-1960s I went to the Village Gate with two friends to hear John Coltrane's Quartet. It was around 1:00 in the morning, definitely the late show. One of my friends asked Coltrane to play his (then) current hit instrumental, "My Favorite Things." By this time, it was almost 2 a.m., and there was a grand total of six or seven people in the club. The piece was 15 to 20 minutes long, depending on Coltrane's inspiration and mood, and halfway into it the light technician started flashing the lights. Clearly, he wanted to go home, and the club was making no money on the show at that point. Coltrane was playing with his eyes closed, and it was impossible to tell whether he was ignoring the flashing lights or simply did not see them. He continued to play for another ten minutes, and then wrapped up the set. It was one of those experiences that set the Village apart from more commercial parts of town, where a club manager or owner would have shut down the show for obvious economic reasons. In the Village there were still opportunities for an artist to be an artist. Even if it irritated the light man.

Currently the property consists of co-op luxury apartments, a smaller basement space featuring an eclectic club called Le Poisson Rouge, and a CVS pharmacy.

165, CAFÉ RAFIO

Rafio was a '60s coffeehouse co-owned and managed by Ronald Von Ehmsen. Von Ehmsen was planning to expand the café, so he tried to evict a tenant in the building named Simone Pepe. He sent an eviction notion to Pepe, who responded by shooting and killing him. Von Ehmsen was a long-hair and Pepe was an older Italian man, and in a sense this incident expressed the tensions between the "native" Italian American population and the encroaching beatniks, who were seeking economic opportunities in the Village. Incidentally, Dylan tried to get a booking at Rafio, but Von Ehmsen turned him away because he didn't like Bob's music.

This tension between the old and new Village population was often present, although it only occasionally erupted into violent confrontations. In 1965 I went out to dinner with my mother at a small restaurant called David's on MacDougal Street, close to where the Commons was located. The staff consisted of David, the owner, and a cook. About a month later the cook and David got into some sort of dispute, and the cook drew a knife and killed David. I have been unable to find any record of David's restaurant or this incident on the net.

THE EDUCATION OF BOB DYLAN

Greenwich Village and its many artists and performers played a key role in broadening Dylan's horizons and making him the singer/songwriter that he would become. When Dylan arrived in New York, he was thrown into an environment that must have appeared both exciting and a bit overwhelming. Because he immediately started playing at the Café Wha?, he was thrown into contact with several Village musicians. In his memoir *Chronicles: Volume One*, he goes into considerable detail about his interactions with Ray Gooch and Chloe Keel. He says that they lived below the Village on Vestry Street below Canal Street. Dylan presents Ray as a critical and cynical libertarian, a military school graduate and attendee at divinity school. He spends less time discussing Chloe, whom he describes as a hatcheck girl at a belly-dancing joint: just the sort of streetwise woman that would impress a nineteen-year-old youth who hasn't even got his own apartment yet. Bob goes into great detail about Gooch and Keel's extensive library of novels, history books, and art books, which he claims to have ardently devoured.

By and large Dylan is fairly straightforward in his descriptions of people and places. Certainly, they are far easier to follow than his novel *Tarantula*. Dylan's songs have frequently stirred up arguments among critics and fans. Are they about real people, friends, enemies, lovers, or ex-lovers? Having said this, no one has ever been able to verify that Gooch and Keel are real people. Dylan mentions that he was introduced to them by his friend Paul Clayton. Since Clayton died in 1967, he is not available to vouch for them. Some critics feel that Gooch and Keel may well be composites of different people Dylan encountered in his early days in New York. (Incidentally, Ray Gooch was a character in a 1942 True Comics book.)

If Dylan invented these people, it is worthwhile to speculate on why he did so. Remember that when Dylan came to New York he changed his name and invented a whole mythological life as an orphan, a runaway, and a rambling hobo, among other identities. It is a reasonable supposition that Dylan is having fun with his readers, creating characters who are, so to speak, more real than actual people could be. Gooch and Keel do not appear in the memoirs of Suze Rotolo and Dave Van Ronk, the two people who probably knew Dylan the best during his New York years.

Robert Shelton, the *New York Times* music critic who was Dylan's first real biographer, pointed out that Dylan did indeed spend nights couch-surfing at the home of Mac and Eve McKenzie, as well as the home of Mel and Lillian Bailey. McKenzie was a longshoreman and Bailey a doctor. Bob used the McKenzies' apartment as a base for songwriting. In some instances, Bob forgot the songs, but the McKenzies kept his lyrics. Dylan would sometimes return to the lyrics and rework the songs to record them. The Baileys liked to make home tapes of Dylan and some of his friends, like Paul Clayton and Ian Tyson, who performed in the duo Ian and Sylvia.*

Suze Rotolo was two years younger than Bob, yet she too was a mentor. When Dylan met here, she was living with her mother and her sister Carla. The

---

*Shelton, *No Direction Home*, 92, 95.

whole family had a background in radical social activism, and Carla was working as an assistant for famed folklorist Alan Lomax and had access to dozens of recordings of roots music artists. Young as Suze was, she had a background in theater and visual arts, and she brought Bob along to arts museums and to theatrical performances. She also worked for CORE, the Congress of Racial Equality.

184–186, CAFÉ FIGARO

John Mitchell, who founded the Gaslight, opened Café Figaro in 1958. Figaro was almost the ultimate hangout in the Village. There was an endless supply of coffee and luminaries like Bob Dylan and his road manager, Victor Maymudes, among others, engaged in long chess games at the venue. A half hour's respite at the club would likely provide the careful listener with lots of information about what artist had just snagged a recording deal or an exciting tour opportunity.

18. Café Figaro.

My favorite Figaro story was told to me by musician Barry Kornfeld. Barry played excellent banjo and guitar, and was one of a half dozen musicians in the Village who made a living playing on other people's records. He has had an interesting and varied music career, shepherding holy blues artist Reverend Gary Davis to folk clubs, playing in Dave Van Ronk's jug band, playing on numerous folk-pop albums, and producing records for Epic, a subsidiary of Columbia Records. Barry recently recounted this story to me. I have seen it in print in several books about Bob Dylan, but rarely with the punchline that Barry revealed to me.

Barry was friendly with Bob Dylan and Dave Van Ronk, and in Dylan's early New York years, Barry participated in the Kettle of Fish gatherings and in the camaraderie of the Village coffee shops. One day Barry, Dylan, and several of their mutual friends were gathered drinking coffee at Figaro. They got to talking about Jack Elliott, who had recently returned to the United States after spending several years touring in Europe. One of the people at the table asked Dylan if he knew who Jack Elliott actually was. Jack was known as a Woody Guthrie disciple who had spent some time as a rodeo cowboy. Bob said that he didn't really know much about Jack. His friends then informed Bob that in fact Elliott's real name was Elliot Adnopoz, and that his father was a very successful Jewish doctor in Brooklyn. Dylan could hardly contain himself, and burst out in uproarious laughter. As the conversation moved to other subjects, Barry would turn to Dylan every few minutes and whisper "Adnopoz" in his ear. Every time Dylan heard the name, he burst out laughing. Of course, Dylan himself had changed his name from Zimmerman to Dylan, to re-create his own image from the son of a midwestern Jewish furniture store owner to something more exotic. Because both Dylan and Arlo Guthrie became musicians when Woody Guthrie was incurably ill, they both essentially adopted Elliott's performing mannerisms, which Elliott had picked up during the time when Woody was healthy and frequently performing.

Two of the people who hung out at Figaro were beat novelist Jack Kerouac and composer and musician David Amram. By the time Bob Dylan arrived in New York, Figaro was swarmed by tourists and visitors who were curious to check out the Village beatniks. Kerouac wrote that many of these visitors wore black clothes, had grown goatees, and were carrying knapsacks. Many had copies of Kerouac's novel *On the Road*, and others carried books by Jean-Paul Sartre, Albert Camus, and Dylan Thomas. The young women wore "black fishnet stockings, black skirts and tight-fitting black sweaters," Kerouac said. "It's like Catholic school, everyone's in uniform."*

---

*David Amram, *Offbeat: Collaborating with Kerouac* (New York: Routledge, 2008).

The walls of the coffeehouse had photos of Amram, Kerouac, jazz great Charlie "Bird" Parker, Thelonious Monk, and Miles Davis. Kerouac remarked that "we're like tourists in a museum about ourselves." Amram added, "they thought Jack and I were two old unemployed dudes from Elizabeth, New Jersey, trying to score." After Kerouac and Amram performed a poem with music, a patron from Ohio told them that they needed to learn how to dress and act to fit into the Village scene. "He'd read up on it in a how-to-be-a beatnik book," Kerouac quipped. Kerouac is long gone, but Amram continues to play music at the age of 91.

The café moved once, and then closed in 2008. The location of the original Café Figaro is now a fast-food place. Currently there are plans afoot to open the café in its original location.

196, THE LITTLE RED SCHOOL HOUSE

Elisabeth Irwin began teaching in the New York public schools around 1916. When the public schools frowned on her efforts to devise a more individualized curriculum, she founded her own school, the Little Red School House, in 1921. During the mid-late 1940s, future banjo artist Eric Weissberg took music lessons at the school from music teacher Charity Bailey, who recorded children's songs for Folkways Records. He also took some banjo lessons from Pete Seeger, whom the school sometimes employed. Mary Travers, of Peter, Paul and Mary, was a student at the school's upper division, Elisabeth Irwin High School, which was located at 40 Charlton Street. Other alumni of the Little Red School House include Robert de Niro, Angela Davis, and Seeger's future wife, Toshi.

259, ZITO'S BAKERY

From 1924 to 2004 well-informed Villagers, including Bob Dylan and his girlfriend Suze Rotolo, frequently showed up at this bakery as the fresh hot bread emerged from Zito's ovens. The bakery was featured in the 1939 photo book *Changing New York* by Berenice Abbott.

273, MATT UMANOV GUITARS

Matt Umanov originally worked for Marc Silber (see 319–321 Sixth Avenue), and then opened his own guitar shop. Initially it was in the East Village, and eventually at 273 Bleecker Street. Matt stopped selling guitars in 2017, but he still operates a repair facility and sells a small number of quality guitars on consignment. He also maintains a web site that contains fascinating information about guitars and his own colorful history. Umanov sold guitars to Bob Dylan and many other famous musicians over the years, and his employee, Zeke Schein, uncovered a rare and somewhat controversial photo of famed Delta blues man Robert Johnson with his friend Johnny Shines. Counting this photo, there are only four known photos of Johnson.

70 BEDFORD STREET

Many of the streets in the Village are primarily residential. Bedford Street is just east of Bleecker, and runs from Sixth Avenue to Christopher Street. Paul (Noel) Stookey of Peter, Paul and Mary bought an abandoned factory building on Bedford for $38,000 in 1962 and turned it into his family home. When Noel first showed his wife Elizabeth the building, he asked what she thought of it. She replied that the building should be torn down! A few doors away lived Bill Schwartau, who was the audio engineer of the first three Peter, Paul and Mary albums. Stookey's home had a colorful history. Previous inhabitants included counterfeiters, a water softening factory, and a furniture shop. In 2003 Stookey embarked on a year-long remodel of the building.

4

Washington Square Park, Sixth Avenue, and Sheridan Square

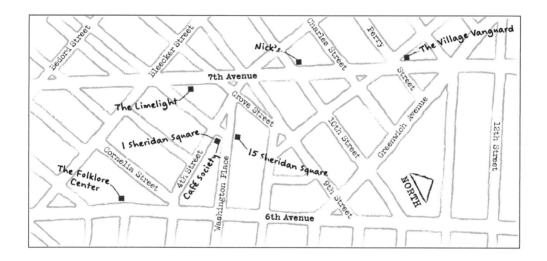

Washington Square Park is a rectangle at the base of Fifth Avenue, between Mac-Dougal Street and University Place (called Washington Square West and Washington Square East when they border the park). Starting in the 1940s, folksingers gathered in the park to perform music on Sunday afternoons. By the time Bob Dylan arrived in New York City, dozens of amateur, semi-professional, and occasionally even well-known folksingers would gather in the Square to sing and play. This attracted many tourists and fans, and young men and women looking to find friendship or romance in a reasonably safe setting.

A fair number of the musicians who gathered in the Square went on to enjoy lifelong careers as professional musicians. Among these musicians were John Sebastian, who founded the successful rock band The Lovin' Spoonful and who grew up in

19. Banjo player in Washington Square Park. Library of Congress, Prints and Photographs Division.

the Village, mandolin virtuoso David Grisman, blues guitarist and instruction book author Stefan Grossman, and studio musician Eric Weissberg, who was a member of The Tarriers, and whose hit instrumental record "Dueling Banjos" became the best-selling banjo recording ever made. (Weissberg's group Deliverance backed up Dylan on the original sessions for his *Blood on the Tracks* album.) Other musicians were often in attendance, like Happy Traum and his brother Artie, Maria D'Amato, early bluegrass banjo player Roger Sprung, versatile instrumentalist Paul Prestopino, and Johnny Herald, the lead singer of the early urban bluegrass group The Greenbriar Boys. Marshall Brickman could often be found playing with his good friend Eric Weissberg. Marshall went on to a successful career writing for films and theatrical works. According to June Skinner Sawyers's book *Bob Dylan: New York*, John Sebastian recalls playing with Dylan in the Park, and Bob even wrote, but did not complete, a song called "Down at Washington Square." Musicians tended to gather in groups according to their stylistic preferences. There were the bluegrass musicians, the blues musicians, musicians performing Israeli music and dancers, and others who tried to enlist the crowd in sing-alongs. There was even an older Italian gentleman who played Italian songs on a bowl-shaped mandolin.

When the Kingston Trio and other pop-folk groups became increasingly popular, the crowds grew larger. The Square is bordered by many apartment buildings that house permanent residents, and some of these people began to protest the noise levels and general proliferation of abandoned food containers and other unsightly garbage that the event left in its wake. The city government was also suspicious of any large-scale gatherings, and concerned about damaging what green space the park contained. In 1961 the local homeowners' group the Washington Square Association complained to the New York City Department of Parks and Recreation about the hundreds of young people gathering at the fountain in the park. Some onlookers felt that the real complaint revolved around the presence of racially mixed couples, especially black men and white women. The commission responded by attempting to limit the number of musicians and requiring them to get permits from the city.

20. Roger Sprung, John Cohen, Mike Seeger, and other musicians, playing in Washington Square. Photo: Sound Associates. From the Ronald D. Cohen Collection #20239, Southern Folklife Collection, The Wilson Library, University of North Carolina at Chapel Hill.

They attempted to ban bongo drums and to limit the hours of performance from 2 to 5 p.m. Because many of the bongo players were black, this was regarded by many as an attempt to limit the presence of black performers in the park.

The city then banned all music in the park. Izzy Young, the owner of the Folklore Center, organized a protest demonstration that drew several hundred people to the park. The demonstrators gathered at the fountain to sing Woody Guthrie's song "This Land Is Your Land" and "The Star-Spangled Banner." Village Gate owner Art D'Lugoff lectured the police about free speech. Parks commissioner Newbold Morris denounced the folk movement for attracting elements from the Bronx to the Village and a committee called the Committee to Preserve the Dignity and Beauty of Washington Square Park was formed to support his stance. Another active supporter of the protest was the Reverend Howard Moody, who had turned the Judson Memorial Church on the south side of Washington Square Park into a major presenter and supporter of theater, music, art, and dance. Moody even founded the Right to Sing Committee, which held its own rally, attended by two thousand people. The police were present, but took no action against the rally.*

During the protests that came to be called the "Washington Square Riots," one hapless autoharp player was arrested and eventually the police waded into the crowd, beat up some of the demonstrators, and arrested many others over a two-hour period. After a considerable amount of media publicity, Morris fought the battle in the courts and achieved a temporary victory. Mayor Robert Wagner then overruled his parks commissioner and reinstated the permits. In a move possibly designed to save face, he continued the ban on bongos.

The Sunday afternoon gatherings presented various opportunities for both local musicians and assorted performers of all kinds. I recall an African American performer who dressed up in cowboy regalia and would do roping tricks in the Square. His belt had the letters "Lightning" stenciled on it. There was also a very tall and overweight "Jewish cowboy" named Tex Konig who hung out in the Square, and who went on to some fame as an actor in Hollywood before moving to Toronto. One of his acting roles was in a film called *The Freshman,* with Marlon Brando and Matthew Broderick, and he also appeared in the films *Billy Madison* and *Head Office.* Konig was also a guitarist; he oddly played a small nylon string guitar that was quite a contrast to his large body. He had a black beard and black bushy eyebrows, which added a bit of panache to an already-large presence. Konig loved Chinese food, and one of his ploys was to invite friends to share a Chinese meal with him

*Heylin, *The Double Life of Bob Dylan*, 41–42.

in New York's Chinatown. At the end of the meal, he would split the bill with his new "friends." Unbeknownst to them, Tex had arrived a half hour earlier and had earlier wolfed down several courses of food before their arrival. Consequently, the friends' share turned out to be significantly larger than they expected!

Sixth Avenue (Avenue of the Americas)

MacDougal Street is located between Fifth Avenue on the east and Sixth Avenue on the west. Sixth Avenue is also known as the Avenue of the Americas. Sixth Avenue was not exactly a place to hang out, but it housed many commercial enterprises, including a shoe store and various restaurants. A great many of these establishments are no longer in business.

319–321 SIXTH AVENUE, THE FOLKLORE CENTER (FROM 1965)

The most important Sixth Avenue address to Dylan was 319-21 Sixth Avenue at Third Street, During the early 1960's a guitar player and luthier named Marc Silber had moved from Ann Arbor, Michigan to Berkeley, California. He was mentored by legendary luthier Jon Lundberg, who had developed a number of innovative repair techniques. In the course of his travels, Marc had met Israel Young, and they agreed that if Marc could open a guitar repair shop, the two businesses could be mutually beneficial to one another. Marc opened his store on Sixth Avenue in 1963. Meanwhile Izzy's rent kept escalating, and in 1965 he moved the Folklore Center to the building next door to Marc's shop.

By that time, the interest in folk instruments had greatly surpassed the market for books about music. Marc quickly developed a reputation as the go-to person in the Village to get an instrument repaired, or to simplify identify instruments that were obscure or even had no brand name on the instrument.

In 1973 Izzy Young closed the Folklore Center and moved to Sweden, and Marc closed his shop and traveled in various parts of the world, and Fretted Instruments was transformed into a music school, teaching guitar and banjo lessons. Jack Baker acquired the store and he employed several teachers who became famous in their own right. This included banjoist Bill Keith and guitarists Russ Barenberg, Stefan Grossman, Rick Schoenberg, and Happy Traum. Although the original shop is gone, Jack continues to teach guitar and banjo lessons nearby. Bill Keith became famous as a bluegrass banjo stylist, Stefan has written dozens of instructional books on blues guitar, Barenberg is well-known as an excellent flat-pick guitarist, and Happy

Traum founded a company called Homespun Tapes that offers dozens of instructional lessons on fiddle, banjo, guitar, and other instruments. Rick Schoenberg developed a reputation as a ragtime guitar player, and he designs guitars and has his own quality guitar shop located in the Bay Area in Tiburon, California. Today, Marc Silber sells guitars in Berkeley, designs both steel string and classical guitars, and performs music primarily in the Berkeley area.

DYLAN'S MANAGERS: ALBERT GROSSMAN

Folk music had really only become a business with the success of The Weavers in the early 1950s. After The Weavers were blacklisted for alleged connections with the Communist Party, there was little impetus to represent folk singers on the part of personal managers. When the Kingston Trio hit the market with their 1958 hit record "Tom Dooley," it became plausible that folk music could make money for presenters, agents, and managers. Subsequent hit records and successful albums by such artist as The Brothers Four, Harry Belafonte, and Peter, Paul and Mary drew the interest of entrepreneurs.

According to intrepid Dylan author Clifford Heylin, Dylan auditioned for manager and music publisher Harold Leventhal. Leventhal was the co-manager of The Weavers, and had an extensive background as a song plugger and booking agent, but the audition apparently did not lead to either a publishing contract or an offer from Leventhal to manage him. Most of the major personal managers in New York stayed away from folk singers, because they did not believe there was much money to be made from them. A sort of second line of managers emerged, including Roy Silver, Herb Gart, and Arthur Gorson. Silver convinced Bob to sign with him as a manager. His most significant act as a manager was to bring Bob to Artie Mogull, a long-term music publishing executive who was working at Witmark Music. Dylan had previously signed a deal with another publisher, but Dylan, with "some help from his friends," was able to get out of that contract.

But Dylan's most significant manager in the '60s was Chicago-born Albert Grossman. Grossman got into the night club business by opening a venue in Chicago called the Gate of Horn. In 1959 Grossman partnered with George Wein to establish the Newport Folk Festival. In 1960 Grossman sold his share of the Gate of Horn and moved to New York City. His early clients included Bob Gibson, Hamilton Camp, and Odetta. Grossman developed the idea of a sort of a more bohemian Kingston Trio. He was managing Peter Yarrow, and after some experimentation and false starts, Noel (Paul) Stookey and Mary Travers joined Peter to form the hit group Peter, Paul and Mary. Stookey had been playing at the MacDougal Street coffeehouses, and introduced Dylan to Al Grossman.

Grossman quickly realized that he could realize large revenues from Bob Dylan as a songwriter. He in effect harnessed Dylan's "rough" sound through Peter, Paul and Mary's recordings. Grossman made a deal with Artie Mogull to form a publishing company whose ownership was split between Grossman and Witmark. When Peter, Paul and Mary recorded "Blowin' in the Wind" and other Bob Dylan songs, Grossman received income from the trio's recordings because he was their personal manager and received revenue from Dylan as a songwriter through his management contract with Dylan, and, unknown to Bob, also was receiving income from Witmark as their co-publisher.

Sheridan Square/The West Side

Sheridan Square is located at the intersection Seventh Avenue and West Fourth Street. It was a center of jazz clubs and theaters that all had an influence on the young Dylan.

1 SHERIDAN SQUARE, APARTMENT BUILDING/CAFÉ SOCIETY

One Sheridan Square is an apartment building whose history goes back to the original four-story building built in 1834. Today it is an eight-story condominium complex. When Bob Dylan arrived in New York, it was virtually a folk music rooming house. Bob Dylan's girlfriend Suze Rotolo lived there with her older sister, Carla, and her mother. So did Miki Isaacson, an intrepid folk music fan who transformed her one-bedroom apartment into a folk music crash pad. Dylan, Peter Yarrow, Jack Elliott, and Scottish singer Jean Redpath were among the various folk singers who crashed on her floor. She kept bedrolls and sleeping bags available for her seemingly endless stream of visitors and there was a communal refrigerator available.

The cellar of the building evolved from a restaurant to the supper club Café Society, founded in 1937 by Barney Josephson. Josephson deliberately sought to erode New York's racial barriers, encouraging a mixed-race audience to attend performances by such notable jazz musicians as Mary Lou Williams, Art Tatum, and Big Joe Turner, and folk-blues singer Josh White. The club's motto was "The wrong place for the right people." Opening night at the club featured a young singer named Billie Holiday, who then enjoyed a nine-month residency there. Josephson capped his impetus toward racial equality by booking black blues and folk singer Josh White with white diva Libby Holman. Such interracial acts were virtually unknown at the time.

During the McCarthy period in American politics, Josephson's brother, who was an "out" member of the Communist Party, was called to testify before the House Un-American Activities Committee in 1947. Josephson himself was red-baited by conservative newspaper columnists. The audience at the club dwindled, and Josephson closed the club in 1950. However, this did not conclude Josephson's relationship with jazz and Greenwich Village.

After he closed Café Society, Josephson established a small chain of restaurants in Midtown Manhattan called The Cookery. In 1969 he consolidated his holdings into a single restaurant, located at Eighth Street and University Place. He resumed presenting music in the new location, and booked such jazz musicians as Teddy Wilson and Nelly Lutcher. In 1977, he booked eighty-two-year-old blues diva Alberta Hunter. Hunter had been a well-known blues singer during the 1920s, but had left music for a nursing career from 1961 to 1977. Hunter proved to be a sensation, and remained at the club until she suffered a fall in 1984. The club closed soon afterward, but in 2003 an off-Broadway show *Cookin' at the Cookery: The Music and Times of Alberta Hunter* recaptured this magical time.

The Café Society began a new life as One Sheridan Square Theatre, only to return to its nightclub history as a the Haven, a gay dance club, during the late 1960s. The club became a victim of the 1969 riots at the Stonewall Bar; in 1970 the police raided the Haven and destroyed much of the club's equipment during the melee. The club then once again became a theater, home of Charles Ludlam's Ridiculous Theatrical Company.

15 SHERIDAN SQUARE

After Dave Van Ronk's divorce from Terri Thal, his first wife, he lived at 15 Sheridan Square. Guitarist-banjoist Barry Kornfeld also moved into this building. Van Ronk became known as the Mayor of MacDougal Street, and the Coen Brothers' *Inside Llewyn Davis* was partially derived from his memoir, co-authored by blues scholar Elijah Wald.

21. Dave Van Ronk, 1968. Photo: Diana Jo Davies. Ralph Rinzler Folklife Archives and Collections, Diana Davies Collection, Smithsonian Center for Folklife and Cultural Heritage.

91 SEVENTH AVENUE SOUTH, THE LIMELIGHT

The Limelight opened in 1954 as a coffeehouse/restaurant with a photography gallery in the back room. Because of the photo studio, famed photographers Weegee, Walker Evans, Lisette Model, and Robert Frank were among the patrons. Limelight patrons included actors and actresses from nearby Village theaters and professors from The New School and NYU. The Village Voice even held its first theater awards ceremony there in 1956. Original owner Helen See sold the club to Manny Roth and Les Lone of Café Wha? in 1961. It then turned into a Village tourist bar.

From 1964 to 1967, Jean Shepherd broadcast a Saturday night radio show from the bar. Shepherd was a well-known WOR radio personality. In 1956, he had promoted a fictitious book on his radio show that aroused the interest of listener and book publisher Ian Ballantine. When the hoax was revealed to Ballantine, he offered to publish the book, *I, Libertine*, if Shepherd and "co-author" science fiction writer Theodore Sturgeon would write it. Supposedly the book, written in three weeks, sold over two hundred thousand copies. *I, Libertine* is a collectible on the internet, selling for far more than its original thirty-five-cent paperback price.

CORNER 10TH STREET AND SEVENTH AVENUE SOUTH, NICK'S

22. Nick's Jazz Club. Photo: William Gottlieb. Library of Congress, Prints and Photographs Division.

Nick's was a jazz club that featured Dixieland jazz from 1937 until 1963. Famous Dixieland and swing musicians like Muggsy Spanier, Bud Freeman, Eddie Condon, and Benny Carter played there, and songwriter and pianist Fats Waller and trombonist Jack Teagarden would sit in when the mood struck them. By the 1960s the interest in Dixieland had diminished, and in 1963 the club closed, replaced by Your Father's Mustache. That club featured sing-alongs and younger, lesser-known musicians, and was one of a chain of clubs that were operating at the time. It closed in 1976.

178 SEVENTH AVENUE SOUTH, THE VILLAGE VANGUARD

23. Village Vanguard. Photo: Tom Marcello. Creative Commons BY-SA 2.0 License.

The longest-lasting and probably the most important jazz club in the Village was and is the Village Vanguard. Max Gordon opened the club in 1934 on Charles Street and Greenwich Avenue. His original notion was to create a performance space for poets, artists, and musicians. He was denied a cabaret license due to inadequate facilities, and quickly moved the club, purchasing an old speakeasy called the Golden Triangle at 178 Seventh Avenue South. He opened the new club in 1935, changing its name to the Village Vanguard.

Gordon began by presenting poetry and folk music. Village poet, novelist, and eccentric Maxwell Bodenheim read his poetry there, Lead Belly and Josh White sang folksongs, and the Duke of Iron held forth with calypso. On Sunday afternoons distinguished jazz musicians like Lester Young and Ben Webster played, and soon the club began to regularly feature jazz players. In 1949 Gordon hired Pete Seeger to perform, but Seeger countered by offering his whole new group, The Weavers, for the same money that he would have received as a solo artist. After negotiating just how many hamburgers the hungry group was entitled to receive, they settled down to a steady months-long engagement. Arranger-producer Gordon Jenkins became enamored of the group's work, and produced a string of hit records with them, until they were outed as left-wing sympathizers and subsequently blacklisted. By that time, the Vanguard could not really afford to hire the group.

By 1957 jazz dominated the bill, with occasional performances by folk musicians and comics. Miles Davis, the Modern Jazz Quartet, Carmen McRae, and Bill Evans all appeared there, and live recordings by Sonny Rollins, Evans, John Coltrane, and Wynton Marsalis led to continuing popularity for the club. From 1966 to 1990 the Thad Jones-Mel Lewis Orchestra, later renamed as the Vanguard Jazz Orchestra, held forth on Monday nights. In 1989 Max Gordon died, and his wife Lorraine Gordon took over the club. She passed on in 2018, and her daughter Deborah Gordon now operates it.

5

West Fourth Street

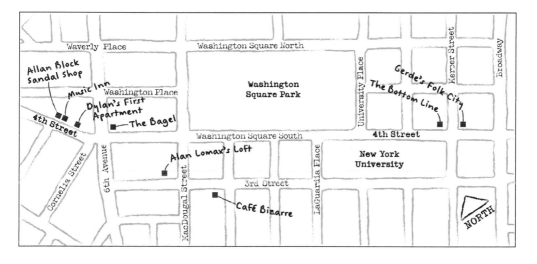

106 WEST THIRD STREET, CAFÉ BIZARRE

Area landlord Rick Allmen opened the Café Bizarre in 1957. Allmen featured beat poets, folk singers, and even comedy—whatever he thought would draw an audience. According to Dave Van Ronk, it was the first Village coffee house to feature folk singers. Van Ronk played there, and he was so outraged by the low wages that Allmen offered, he organized a sort of folk singer's union called the Folksingers Guild. They presented a handful of concerts at various venues in the Village. The concerts featured three or four Guild members, and there was an attempt to rotate the work to avoid favoritism.

121 WEST THIRD STREET, ALAN LOMAX'S LOFT

Alan Lomax (1915–2002) had a long and varied career as a folklorist, author, and occasional performer. Suze Rotolo's sister Carla worked for Alan, and Bob Dylan was therefore able to access some of the recordings that Lomax had made. Lomax had frequent gatherings of musicians at his loft, and Dylan describes seeing Mike Seeger, founding member of the New Lost City Ramblers, there, among others, as he relates in *Chronicles*:

> You might see Roscoe Holcomb or Clarence Ashley or Dock Boggs, Mississippi John Hurt, Robert Pete Williams or even Don Stover and The Lilly Brothers—sometimes, even real live section gang convicts that Lomax would get out of state penitentiaries on passes and bring to New York to do field hollers in his loft. The invitees to these gatherings would most likely be local doctors, city dignitaries, anthropologists, but there'd always be some regular folk there too. I'd been there once or twice.*

Lomax's collection is housed at The Association for Cultural Equity, at 425 East 25th Street in New York City.

FOLKSINGERS GUILD

24. Dave Van Ronk, Bob Yellin, and Roy Berkeley playing together at the Folklore Center. Photo: Sound Associates. From the Ronald D. Cohen Collection #20239, Southern Folklife Collection, The Wilson Library, University of North Carolina at Chapel Hill.

---

*Dylan, *Chronicles: Volume One*, 70.

The Guild was organized by Van Ronk and group of his friends and peers, including Roy Berkeley and future folklorist Roger Abrahams. It held meetings at a loft where guitarist Dick Greenhaus and his wife, dancer Kiki Greenhaus, lived. To build enthusiasm for the Guild, it held several concerts at various Village locations. Because the group never gained any traction outside Greenwich Village, and several of the group's members began to find gigs that paid reasonably well, the organization gradually dissipated.

15 WEST FOURTH STREET, THE BOTTOM LINE

Although the Bottom Line club did not exist during Bob Dylan's early New York years, it was a significant player in the Village nightlife scene from its opening in 1974 until its closing in 2004. The club tended to hire acts in a rock or folk-rock vein, but from time to time it also featured such artists as country-folksinger and guitarist Doc Watson, and such singer-songwriters as Emmylou Harris, Neil Young, and Laura Nyro. New York University was the landlord of the club, and by 2003 the venue owed hundreds of thousands of dollars in rent and other expenses. Owners Allan Pepper and Stan Snadowsky closed the club shortly before they would have been evicted. Bruce Springsteen and Sirius Satellite Radio had offered to pay the club's back rent, but the owners were unable to reach an agreement for a new lease with NYU. Springsteen had played showcases at the club, and felt that it was an important step in his career, and that the club was an important part of Village nightlife.

Dylan would visit the club to hear artists he enjoyed. Paul Oscher, who played with bluesman Muddy Waters, recalls one evening from 1975 when Dylan joined the group on stage:

> We were on a break. Muddy's manager Scott Cameron came into the dressing room and told Muddy "There's a real heavyweight in the house and he wants to sit in on the harmonica, his name is Bob Dylan." So we went back up and Muddy . . . called me up to play a harmonica instrumental. When I finished Dylan walked on the stage and this photo is me handing him a harp and Muddy is introducing him, "Ladies and Gentlemen, I want you to put your hands together for a great harp blower he's one of the best, JOHN Dylan." There was minimal applause then guitarist Bob Margolin whispered to Muddy "Its Bob Dylan, not John."

Then Muddy corrected himself, "I'm sorry Ladies and gentlemen this is BOB DYLAN," and the audience went wild.*

11 WEST FOURTH STREET, GERDE'S FOLK CITY

Folk City was an important venue in the development of Bob Dylan's career, and for the folk revival in general. In 1952 original owner William Gerdes sold his restaurant on West Third Street to three Italian immigrants: Mike Porco, his brother, and their cousin. Four years later the property was replaced by high-rise apartment buildings and Gerdes moved to 11 West Fourth Street. This building had a bar and a dining room that was separated by a partition. The employees were largely members of the Porco family. The city began to tear down buildings near the new location, so Porco added a piano player, and then a trio, to attract an audience separate from local barflies. Porco told author Robbie Wolliver that he paid the musicians $10 each for two or three hours' work.

In 1960 an advertising executive named Tom Prendergast wandered into the Folklore Center on MacDougal Street and proposed to Izzy Young that the two of them open a folk music club in Mike Porco's bar. They worked out a deal with Porco that he could keep all the receipts from the sale of food and drink, and they would assess a cover charge and bring in lights. There was no written contract between them, only a verbal agreement. Young and Prendergast called the club the Fifth Peg, named after the short string on a five-string banjo. Because of Izzy's store the Folklore Center, he already knew most of the folk musicians in New York, and of course virtually all of them were eager to work at a venue where they were actually paid and didn't have to pass a basket around, begging for donations. Izzy quickly booked Ed McCurdy, Brother John Sellers, Tommy Makem and the Clancy Brothers, Carolyn Hester, Brownie McGhee and Sonny Terry, and Theodore Bikel. Although many of these artists are not well known today, at that time they were among the top folk singers in New York. There was a certain amount of friction between the

---

*Paul Oscher, "Muddy Waters, Bob Dylan and Paul Oscher. . . ." Facebook, August 26, 2015, facebook.com/PaulOscherMusic/photos/muddy-waters-bob-dylan-and-paul-oscherthis-photo-was-taken-at-the-bottom-line-in/1699512123610244/. Punctuation has been adjusted for readability.

people at the bar, who mostly wanted to drink and socialize, and the customers who had paid to see the entertainment.

25. Marc Porco, owner of Gerde's Folk City, in 1973. Photo: Diana Jo Davies. Ralph Rinzler Folklife Archives and Collections, Diana Davies Collection, Smithsonian Center for Folklife and Cultural Heritage.

The club closed for a few weeks because Mike claimed that he had to straighten out some problems with the city, but when it reopened somehow the original excitement had died down. Izzy then asked Mike for a percentage of the bar receipts, because the cover charge wasn't producing enough revenue for Tom and Izzy to even break even. Mike replaced the two partners with entrepreneur and booking agent Charlie Rothschild as the club's manager and folk singer Logan English as the MC. I had played at the club with Brownie McGhee and Sonny Terry, and I recall that the folk community was divided in its loyalties. Some supported Izzy, who they felt was sincere and was art-oriented rather than money-oriented; others took the position that Izzy was a great guy but a terrible businessman, so that the split was inevitable. The Fifth Peg name was removed from the club, and life went on.

BOB DYLAN AND FOLK CITY

By the time Bob Dylan appeared at Folk City, on April 11, 1961, as the opening act for John Lee Hooker, Mike Porco was running the club. Mike took a liking to Bob, and told him that he needed to join Local 802, the New York local of the musicians' union. Because Bob was underage, he needed to have someone sign to certify that his application was accurate. Dylan told Mike that he was an orphan, and Mike agreed to vouch for him. He and Bob went to the midtown headquarters of the union, where Mike was friendly with one of the employees.

At the time, to become a member of the union, a musician actually had to pass an audition. The union rep would bring out a piece of sheet music and the musician would then have to read the music. Folk singers were instructed by savvy friends to say that they simply sang and accompanied themselves. When I auditioned, the union man stopped me after I got through one verse of the song I prepared, said OK, asked me for the money, and that was that. I have never read anywhere that Dylan was asked to audition, so I assume Mike's friendship with the union rep enabled Bob to avoid this process.

Bob appeared in various roles at Folk City, including working with guitarist-singer Mark Spoelstra in a duo. Spoelstra was a well-rehearsed twelve-string guitarist, and a smooth singer, so the duo must have presented quite a combination of contrasting sounds. Gradually Bob worked on his repertoire, and on September 29, 1961, he appeared on a bill with the popular local bluegrass group The Greenbriar Boys. Meanwhile Dylan had become friendly with Bob Shelton, who was writing folk music reviews for the *New York Times*. To everyone's surprise, except possibly for Bob, Shelton essentially ignored The Greenbriar Boys and wrote a rave review of Bob's performance, which was effectively the beginning of Bob's major-league career.

In 1978, three new owners took over the booking of Folk City, buying the club two years later. They brought back some of the early performers, like Odetta and Arlo Guthrie, and began to introduce numerous singer-songwriters and even rock acts to the club's audience. By the 1980s more and more rock acts were featured, and a benefit 45th Anniversary Concert was held in 1985. Two years later the club lost its lease, but the owners from time to time presented Folk City concerts all around the country. One of the owners, Robbie Woliver, co-authored a musical based on the history of the club, and he also wrote a book called *Hoot!: A 25-Year History of the Greenwich Village Music Scene.* The book includes many interviews with people who either played at Folk City or attended performances there.

WEST FOURTH STREET AND SIXTH AVENUE, THE BAGEL

In her memoir *A Freewheelin' Time*, Suze Rotolo reports that she and Bob frequently snacked here.

161 WEST FOURTH STREET, DYLAN'S FIRST APARTMENT

26. Location of Dylan's apartment on West Fourth Street.

This was Bob Dylan's first real apartment of his own. He lived with Suze Rotolo in a one-bedroom apartment at this address, moving there in December 1961. Currently the building has seven units, and the average rental costs $4,718 per month; Dylan was paying $60!

JOHN HAMMOND AND DYLAN'S FIRST RECORD CONTRACT

Bob was eager to record his own album, but he had been rejected by Elektra Records owner Jac Holzman, and when Bob attempted to solicit a record deal from Moe Asch at Folkways Records, instead he again met with rejection, this time at the hands of *Sing Out!* editor Irwin Silber. *Sing Out!* and Folkways shared midtown offices, and Bob was unable to contact Asch.

John Hammond was a talent discoverer and record company producer who was responsible for bringing several major figures in the world of jazz and singer-songwriters to national popularity. Among them were jazz singer Billie Holiday, influential modern jazz guitarist Charley Christian, Bob Dylan, Bruce Springsteen, and rock-blues guitarist and singer Stevie Ray Vaughan. Hammond was the great-grandson of Cornelius Vanderbilt, who owned several large shipping companies. He was also an early proponent of racial integration in both music and society.

Hammond was a Yale graduate and a viola player who early on developed a fanatical interest in jazz. Possibly it was the political content of the '50s and '60s folk singers that drew Hammond to that music as well. In 1961 Columbia Records signed Texas folk singer Carolyn Hester. At the time, Columbia was eager to find someone to compete with Joan Baez, who had started recording for Vanguard Records a year earlier. Hester and Dylan had met in Boston, and she invited Bob to play harmonica on her album. Farina was an aspiring writer with a sort of unruly and creative style of playing the dulcimer, and he and Dylan quickly hit it off together.

Hammond came to a pre-production rehearsal that Hester was holding in the Village to hear the band, which consisted of bass player Bill Lee (filmmaker Spike Lee's father) and guitarist Bruce Langhorne. Hammond was fascinated with Dylan, and when he found out that Bob wrote songs, he invited him to come see him at his Columbia Records office. By the end of October, 1961, Hammond had offered Dylan a recording contract. Hammond attended a Dylan show on

September 26th at Folk City. A few days later Robert Shelton wrote a rave review in the *New York Times* of Bob's show. If Hammond had any doubts about the wisdom of signing a twangy-voiced unknown Minnesota émigré to the label, the review solidified the deal.

From Dylan's standpoint, the Columbia contract was almost beyond his wildest dreams. He had originally sought a deal from much smaller independent folk labels, and now he was signed to one of the world's largest record labels. Moreover, Hammond had earlier signed folk singer Pete Seeger, who was suffering through a lengthy blacklist from record labels and television networks. Pete was idolized by virtually all the Village folksingers, who were in awe of a man who was willing to risk a jail term rather than violate his ideals or incriminate his friends. Columbia may have been a major label, but it seemed to be aligned with the ideology of the folk movement.

Progressive or not, Columbia Records was operating a business. Dylan's original contract offered him a 2 percent royalty rate, which would gradually escalate to 3 and then 4 percent. Dylan had very little music business experience, and not surprisingly, he signed the contract based on his faith in John Hammond's integrity. Because Dylan was not yet 21 years old, the company wanted Bob's father to sign the contract as well. Bob told Hammond that his only relative was an uncle in Nevada, and he had no idea of how to contact him. Ultimately this subterfuge allowed Bob's manager to renegotiate the contract.

169 WEST FOURTH STREET, MUSIC INN

Music Inn was one of the places where Bob Dylan liked to hang out. It is still located just west of Sixth Avenue. Dylan used to pop in to listen to new records or to borrow them. The store is an unusual, jam-packed collection of guitars, sitars, and many other stringed instruments. Music stores in New York City tend to come and go, depending on real estate trends and the owners' willingness to adapt to new musical trends and fads. Music Inn has been in operation for over 60 years. In 1958 it was opened as a record shop by Jerry Halpern. Jeff Slatnick, the current owner, first encountered the store when he was searching for sitar strings. He became a part-time employee and the store then began carrying guitars. Jeff's interest in global music brought about the store's entry into the world musical instrument market. He also builds guitars, basses, and sitars.

27. The Music Inn.

171 WEST FOURTH STREET, ALLAN BLOCK SANDAL SHOP

Allan Block was a sandal maker and fiddle player who opened a small shop to sell his wares in 1950. On Saturday afternoons the store was used for folk jam sessions. Participants included many local musicians, but touring musicians would also stop by to join in. Bob Dylan was an occasional participant. Block's daughter Rory developed a career as a singer-songwriter and blues artist. She even recorded a blues instructional album with her friend Stefan Grossman when she was just a teenager. Rory's career continues to the present day. The shop is currently a juice bar.

6

The West Village

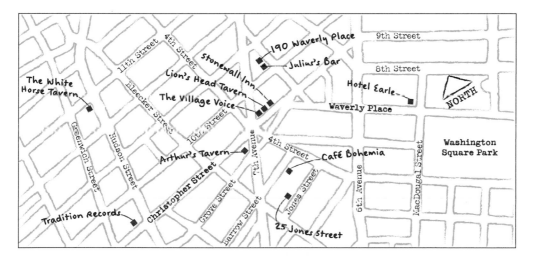

Waverly Place got its name from Sir Walter Scott's 1814 novel *Waverley*, despite its misspelling of the original name. In 1837, 137 Waverly Place was the home of fabled author Edgar Allan Poe. Next door at 139, Edna St. Vincent Millay was in residence in 1917. This literary tradition continues today with the presence of the Writers' Room, a workshop space for authors that opened here in 1985. Waverly Place intersects with Christopher Street where the Stonewall Inn was the site of a 1969 police raid against gay patrons of the bar. This was followed by street riots between gay rights and civil liberties supporters and the New York City police department.

103 WAVERLY PLACE, HOTEL EARLE
(NOW THE WASHINGTON SQUARE HOTEL)

The Hotel Earle was in the heart of the musical action for folk music and singer-songwriters. Many folk singers stayed there while working in New York City.

Among them were Bob Dylan, Jack Elliott—his early mentor for channeling Woody Guthrie—and Peter La Farge. La Farge was the son of Oliver La Farge, novelist and Native American Rights activist. Peter wrote the song "The Ballad of Ira Hayes," about a Native American flag-raiser at Iwo Jima who became a victim of alcohol. The song was a big hit for country artist Johnny Cash. Other celebrities who stayed at the Earl include Ernest Hemingway, Barbra Streisand, Joni Mitchell, John and Michelle Phillips of the Mamas & the Papas, rock-and-roll pioneers Chuck Berry and Bo Diddley, and blues man Albert King. Joan Baez memorialized her time with Bob Dylan at the Earl in her song "Diamonds and Rust."

The hotel dates back to 1902. It was remodeled and renamed the Washington Square Hotel in 1986.

190 WAVERLY PLACE, APARTMENT BUILDING

190 Waverly Place was a building that quickly grew to be a sort of refuge for folk singers seeking reasonable rents. A student of guitarist Barry Kornfeld was a real estate agent, and he rented space to Barry, Dave Van Ronk and his wife Terri Thal, and singer-songwriter-folk singer Patrick Sky. Barry recalls that the rent was $91.60 a month, and the building was rent controlled. This meant that the landlord could only apply for nominal rent increases under New York City law.

Dylan was a frequent visitor and couch surfer at the Van Ronk apartment. Barry also recalled an incident where he was running Eddie Simon's (Paul's brother) Guitar Study Center. Columbia Records publicist Don DeVito "showed up and says grab a mandolin." Barry didn't play much mandolin, and the only mandolin he could find was a National metal model in wretched condition. Nevertheless, he followed Don's instructions and rushed to the Columbia studio where the album *Blood on The Tracks* was bring recorded. As it turned out, Barry never played a note on the session.

159 WEST 10TH STREET
(10TH STREET AND WAVERLY PLACE), JULIUS'S BAR

This bar was opened in 1840 as a grocery store, and was converted to a bar in 1864. During the Prohibition era it was a speakeasy, with seven exit and entrance doors. In 1966 four homophile activists were refused service here, resulting in a 1967 New York Humans Rights Commission decision that compelled bars to serve homosexuals.

This activism was also a response to police harassment of gay customers. Julius's is one of the oldest gay bars in New York City. By the 1950s such prominent gay cultural figures as playwright Tennessee Williams and novelist Truman Capote drank at Julius's, as did bisexual dancer Rudolf Nureyev.

51–53 CHRISTOPHER STREET, THE STONEWALL INN

The Stonewall Inn was a gay restaurant and bar. In 1966 members of the Genovese Family, a famous Mafia family, reconfigured the club as a gay bar. The club had no liquor license so it was a private bottle club. A bouncer would inspect patrons through a peephole in the door. Police were paid off on a weekly basis and the club was the only bar for gay men in the entire city where dancing was allowed. A smaller room in the back was preferred by cross-dressing men. Patrons were white, black, and Hispanic.

There were monthly police raids, but they were usually done early in the evening and often management was tipped off in advance. On June 28, 1969, two policemen and two policewomen entered the bar to gather evidence for the Public Morals Squad waiting outside. Although the raid had been rumored, in this instance there was no advance warning that it was coming. Police entered the bar after 1 a.m., much later than the police raids that the bar owners were used to. They turned off the music and turned on the main lights in the bar. The doors were barred and the police decided to take all 205 patrons to the station. The patrons included gay men, lesbians, and cross-dressers.

As the raid developed, a group of over a hundred people gathered outside the bar to protest, some of whom were Stonewall patrons that the police had released. The original protest was nonviolent, but when a woman was escorted in handcuffs to a police wagon the crowd became violent, and the police knocked a few people to the ground. Soon there were some four hundred people rioting. The police barricaded themselves inside the bar after the rioters threw bottles and debris at them. The riots lasted with varying intensity for five days. They became a catalyst for gay political activism and led to the formation of several gay rights organizations in the United States and England. The bar closed shortly after the riots, but the site has periodically witnessed demonstrations supporting gay rights or commemorating anniversaries of events of significance in the movement for gay rights.

In 1999 the US National Park Service designated the Stonewall Inn on the National register of Historic Places, and in 2016 President Barack Obama designated the site as a national monument. In 2019 New York City Police Commissioner James P. O'Neil issued an apology for police actions in the riot, saying that "the actions taken by the N.Y.P.D. were wrong—plain and simple."*

59 CHRISTOPHER STREET, LION'S HEAD TAVERN

The Lion's Head was originally a coffeehouse on Hudson Street, but by the '60s it was a friendly competitor of the White Horse Tavern. The tavern attracted some of the same people as the Horse drew, notably the Clancy Brothers and Norman Mailer, but it particularly appealed to writers and reporters. Dozens of book jackets by Lion's Head patrons lined the wall. Actress Jessica Lange waitressed there, and writers Pete Hamill, Jimmy Breslin, Lanford Wilson, and Frank McCourt, and actors William Hurt and Bill Murray were frequent patrons. The offices of the *Village Voice* weekly newspaper were located next door, which brought an influx of writers and reporters from it and other New York news outlets. As was the case with the White Horse, the Clancy Brothers frequently sang their Irish revolutionary songs and ballads. Norman Mailer hatched his mayoralty campaign here, and Robert F. Kennedy was an occasional and honored visitor. The bar closed in 1996, and is currently the location of the Kettle of Fish bar, which moved there from MacDougal Street. From its artistic roots, the bar has been transformed into a sports bar for fans of the Green Bay Packers.

61 CHRISTOPHER STREET, THE VILLAGE VOICE

The Village Voice founded in 1955 and quickly established itself as the voice of the Village artistic community and its more recent left-leaning emigrants. Its classified section included listings by bands seeking musicians as well as apartment rentals, all of which were eagerly devoured by Village folkies. The *Voice* had extensive arts coverage, and theater critic Jerry Talmer, filmmaker and critic Jonas Mekas, and rock music critics Robert Christgau and Ellen Willis were among its regular contributors. Each week cartoonist Jules Feiffer drew satirical cartoons, long after

---

*Michael Gold and Derek M. Norman, "Stonewall Riot Apology: Police Actions Were 'Wrong,' Commissioner Admits," *New York Times*, June 6, 2019, www.nytimes.com/2019/06/06/ny region/stonewall-riots-nypd.html.

his success left him no financial reasons to do so. In addition to covering the arts, contributor Wayne Barrett investigated politicians and real estate developers. The *Voice* also instituted the Obie theater awards and annual "Pazz & Jop" music polls. The *Voice* moved its offices several times, including locations at 11th and University Place, Broadway and 13th Street, and 36 Cooper Square.

In later years the *Voice* was acquired by various conglomerates, and laid off some of its best-known staff writers, such as jazz critic and civil liberties columnist Nat Hentoff and music critic Robert Christgau. In 2018 the *Voice* closed, but it currently exists as a website and a quarterly print publication.

131 CHRISTOPHER STREET, TRADITION RECORDS

Guggenheim family heiress Diane Hamilton founded Tradition Records in 1956. Patrick "Paddy" Clancy of the Irish folk group the Clancy Brothers operated the label, and the Clancy Brothers and their friend Tommy Makem became its most popular artists. The label also recorded Glenn Yarbrough, the lead singer of the pop-folk group the Limeliters, Odetta, John Jacob Niles, and various British artists. Odetta was a client of Dylan's manager, Al Grossman, and Bob was a fan of the Clancy Brothers, spending quite a bit of time at the White Horse Tavern, where they often held forth.

DYLAN THE HITMAKER

In the summer of 1964 I attended the Newport Folk Festival. This was the year before Dylan turned to electric instruments. I was in the audience when Dylan performed his own version of "Blowin' in the Wind." Ticket sales hadn't gone too well that year, and a group of sailors were given free tickets to the show. I was sitting next to two of them. One was annoyed by Dylan's twangy singing and he turned to the other, and said something to the effect of "What is this garbage?"

The other sailor looked at him and said "That's the guy who wrote that song for Peter, Paul and Mary." The first sailor immediately quieted down and concentrated on listening to Bob. It was then that I realized that the era of Bob Dylan, hit artist, had begun.

15 BARROW STREET, CAFÉ BOHEMIA

Café Bohemia was originally a restaurant and bar, opening in 1949. Bebop legend Charlie Parker was living across the street with beat poet Ted Joans in 1955. Parker's career was in decline, and he offered to play for nothing but free drinks, so owner Jimmy Garofolo booked him. Before the booking began, Parker died, but because of his death considerable publicity was generated for the club. Many legendary jazz groups played the club, including the Miles Davis Quintet and the original version of Art Blakey's Jazz Messengers. Bass player Oscar Pettiford even wrote the tune "Bohemia after Dark" to celebrate the club. At one point the little-known but critically regarded pianist Herbie Nichols was the intermission pianist. Several live albums were recorded at the club.

A near legendary but true story about sax player Cannonball Adderley is part of the club's history. The then-unknown Adderley was spotted carrying a saxophone case by band leader Pettiford. The band was missing a saxophone player because saxophonist Jerome Richardson had accepted a record date and was unavailable. Adderley created a sensation, and soon was playing with his own group at the Bohemia before joining the Miles Davis Sextet.

The club closed in 1960, but reopened once again in 2019.

25 JONES STREET

This is where the famous cover for Dylan's album *The Freewheelin' Bob Dylan* was shot. The cover features a photo of Bob with Suze Rotolo.

57 GROVE STREET, ARTHUR'S TAVERN

Arthur's has been featuring jazz and blues music since 1937. It offers a mix of jazz, blues, rhythm and blues, and Dixieland music, seven days a week. Monday night is reserved for Dixieland jazz, and there is also a piano bar.

567 HUDSON STREET, THE WHITE HORSE TAVERN

The White Horse is located close to the waterfront. It was founded in 1880 as a longshoreman's bar, and the grandfather of the bar's owner, James Munson, was a boss at the docks. The bar was a gathering spot for radical dockworkers and Merchant

28. White Horse Tavern. Library of Congress, Prints and Photographs Division.

Marine members through the 1930s and '40s. There were street fights outside the bar between various radical and conservative factions of the various unions. During the McCarthy period in American politics in the 1950s, there were attacks on the Horse between conservative seamen and the blacklisted longshoremen who hung out at the tavern. There was even a custom of the left-leaning seamen singing old radical songs, which sometimes provoked fights with conservative bar customers.

The famous Welsh poet Dylan Thomas loved to frequent the Horse. He was a regular visitor to the United States and often drank copiously at a table where young people hung out, awaiting some poetic words from the master. In the fall of 1953 he sank into a coma after two long nights of drinking at the tavern. This became part of the legendary history of the bar. A portrait of Thomas hangs in the middle room of the tavern.

Novelist and Village character Norman Mailer was another writer who found a home at the White Horse, and during the early 1950s he and novelist Vance Bourjaily held regular Sunday afternoon writers' gatherings there. British actor Richard Burton also visited when in New York. Black novelist James Baldwin and socialist author and theoretician Michael Harrington were other attendees. Jack Kerouac was once thrown out of the bar for misbehaving, and the late great gonzo journalist Hunter Thompson was also a patron.

By the time Bob Dylan arrived in New York, the Clancy Brothers and Tommy Makem had become regulars at the bar. They were all actors as well as singers, and this attracted yet another group of patrons to the establishment. Singer-novelist Richard Farina and singer Mary Travers also were attendees. Village activist and preservationist Jane Jacobs was another supporter. Dylan and his girlfriend Suze Rotolo enjoyed the singing and the atmosphere at the Horse and became enthusiastic participants. Periodically, when moved, the Clancy Brothers would break into song.

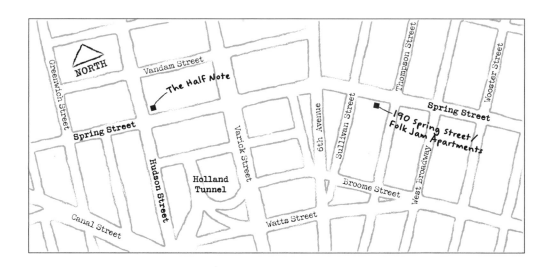

190 SPRING STREET, FOLK JAM APARTMENTS

South of the Village was an apartment building where a few folk singers and fans lived. On Sunday evenings there were regular jam sessions. The different apartments were basically divided into different music factions. There was the bluegrass apartment, the ballad apartment, and so forth. Future folklorist Roger Abrahams, professional folk singer Paul Clayton, and Village folk singer Gina Glaser were often in attendance.

HUDSON AND SPRING STREETS, THE HALF NOTE

The Half Note was downtown from the West Village, but from 1957 to 1971 it featured several modern jazz players. Owner Mike Canterino knew saxophonist Cannonball Adderley from their service in the Navy. Many live albums were recorded at the Half Note by such artists as guitarist Wes Montgomery and saxophonist Lee Konitz.

7

North to Midtown Manhattan

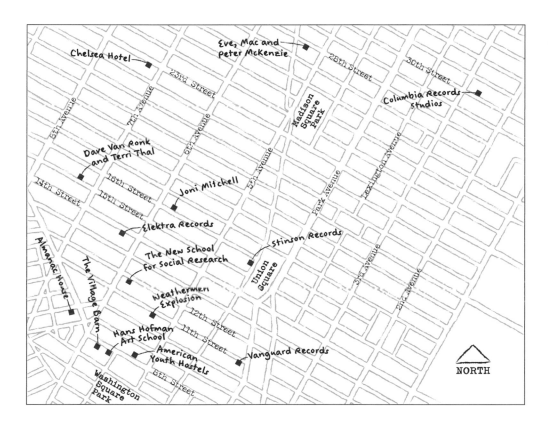

North of Washington Square Park/Union Square

11 WEST EIGHTH STREET, AMERICAN YOUTH HOSTELS

Folk singers would hold jam sessions at the American Youth Hostels offices on Sunday late afternoons, after the festivities at Washington Square Park had concluded. Many of the park's participating musicians would grab a quick sandwich and drift over to AYH, which was only a few blocks from Washington Square. Although this was a relatively loose gathering, it enabled performers to do solo work. This was almost impossible in the square, due to the noise levels of both other musicians and traffic.

38 WEST EIGHTH STREET, HANS HOFMANN SCHOOL OF FINE ARTS

Hans Hofmann was a renowned painter and teacher. He established his own art school at this address. Artists Mark Rothko, Robert Motherwell, and Clyfford Still opened their own Subjects of the Artists School in a loft at 35 East Eighth Street.

52 WEST EIGHTH STREET, THE VILLAGE BARN

The Village Barn was a unique music establishment for bohemian Greenwich Village. It opened in 1930 and was a family business that was passed down to various members of the Horowitz (Horton) family. An NBC network television country show was broadcast there 1949–1950. The television show also featured square dancing and cornball audience participation features like potato sack races. Crooner Rudy Vallée discovered comedienne Judy Canova at the Barn, and '50s pop singer Don Cornell got his start at the club. Many of the performers, like Piute Pete and Pappy Howard and His Tumbleweed Gang, would have been unknown to the Village's hip residents, but were appealing to tourists.

The Barn closed in 1967, and it briefly became a rock venue called the Generation Club. Rock legend Jimi Hendrix and his manager Mike Jeffries bought the club and turned it into Electric Lady Recording Studios shortly before Hendrix's death.

130 WEST TENTH STREET, ALMANAC HOUSE

In 1941 a group of folk singers who specialized in politically oriented songs moved into a sort of folk music commune that became known as Almanac House. The group was an outgrowth of a group of singers who called themselves the Almanac Singers. Among the group members were Pete Seeger, Lee Hays, Bess Lomax—the sister of famed folk music collector Alan Lomax—and future screenwriter Millard Lampell. Others in residence were Pete Hawes and Woody Guthrie. The Almanacs were essentially the first folk revival group. There were few formal rehearsals, and the musicians who went out on jobs might include any of the people listed above, plus accordion player Sis Cunningham, her husband Gordon Friesen, famed folklorist Alan Lomax, Tom Glazer, Burl Ives, Earl Robinson, Lead Belly, and Josh White—whoever was available.

Before America entered World War II, the group followed the Communist Party line of opposing American participation in the war, even recording an album. They also recorded two albums of folk songs. After the war ended, Pete Seeger and Lee Hays formed the bedrock of The Weavers, who were the first American folk group to achieve mass popularity.

18 WEST 11TH STREET, WEATHERMEN EXPLOSION

In 1970 some of the leaders the radical Weathermen movement were staying at this brownstone building when a bomb accidentally exploded. At the time, Dustin Hoffman, the well-known actor, lived next door and was spotted leaving his home carrying a painting. Several of the people staying in the house became hunted fugitives—they were eventually found and served prison terms. The Weathermen took their name from the Dylan song "Subterranean Homesick Blues." It contains the lyric "you don't need a weatherman to know which way the wind blows."

80 EAST 11TH STREET, VANGUARD RECORDS

Vanguard was founded in 1947 by two brothers, Maynard and Seymour Solomon. Both brothers were serious fans of classical music, but because of their sympathies for left-wing causes they issued recordings by The Weavers. Gradually the label recorded more and more folk artists. Joan Baez was far more successful than any previous Vanguard artist, and the label also recorded Native American singer Buffy Sainte-Marie, Canadian duo Ian & Sylvia, and the Jim Kweskin Jug Band. The 1962 hit record "Walk Right In," an old jug band song recorded by The Rooftop Singers, proved to be a one-off hit, although the label continued to do projects with musician and songwriter Erik Darling, who had cofounded the group with his friend Bill Svanoe. Like Elektra, Vanguard dipped its toe in rock-and-roll waters with the band Country Joe and the Fish, but their popularity was more as a niche group than one that had mass appeal. The label was sold to the Welk Music group in 1985.

66 WEST 12TH STREET, THE NEW SCHOOL FOR SOCIAL RESEARCH

The New School was founded in 1919 as an experimental school with no grades or degrees. In 1933 it actively recruited Nazi refugees in a "University in Exile." During the 1930s various artists and social scientists taught here, including composers Aaron Copland, John Cage, and Henry Cowell. Cowell produced many recordings for Folkways Records of music from all corners of the world. Paul Simon's brother Eddie established the Guitar Study Center in the early 1970s. It later became integrated into the curriculum of The New School. These days The New School boasts a strong jazz instruction program.

110 WEST 14TH STREET, ELEKTRA RECORDS

Elektra Records began in 1950 in Jac Holzman's college dormitory at St. John's College in Annapolis, Maryland. Jac was the son of a successful New York doctor, and he had developed interests in audio as well as classical and folk music. To fund his label, he used $300 from his bar mitzvah bank account, and another $300 from college classmate Paul Rickoff. At the advice of a dean at St. John's, he decided to take a year off and try his luck in New York City. He rented a space for $100 a month and opened a record store, the Record Loft, in 1952. After issuing a classical album by composer John Gruen, Elektra's second record was an album by Kentucky folksinger Jean Ritchie. During the next few years Holzman recorded singer and actor Theo Bikel, instrumentalist and singer Tom Paley, blues and folk singer Josh White, folk singer and Dylan rival Phil Ochs, singer-songwriter Tom Paxton, as well as Eric Andersen and singer-songwriter Judy Collins. Elektra was one of several labels that turned Bob Dylan down. Given that Holzman was a bit of a perfectionist when it came to sound and performances, Dylan's early casual style of recording probably would have been a poor fit for the label. In 1964 Holzman founded a budget classical label called Nonesuch. Initially the label released European classical music imports in attractive packages. Soon he added well-recorded albums from different parts of the world. By 1967, the label began recording rock bands, scoring a big success with The Doors. Elektra was acquired by the Kinney Corporation, and eventually became a division of Warner Records. Jac became a consultant to Warner Records, and his book 1998 *Follow the Music* details his story and the history of the label.

219 WEST 15TH STREET, DAVE VAN RONK AND TERRI THAL

When Dave and Terri got married, this was their first apartment. Bob Dylan often visited and crashed on their couch.

Union Square

Union Square is located just north of the Village. It extends from 14th Street to 17th Street and is located at the point where Broadway and Fourth Avenue almost join together. The square has a long and colorful history, including mid-nineteenth-century concert halls and the Union Square Theatre. There was also a dark underbelly of brothels and gambling dens. The square had a long and storied history as a gathering place for speakers to mount soap boxes and deliver speeches about political and social issues. Generally, these speeches reflected left-wing viewpoints. Sometimes the square was used as an endpoint for political rallies that took place in other parts of Manhattan. These days there are numerous restaurants and a farmers' market, and there are occasional political rallies and musical performances.

Although the square is not actually located in the Village, the spirit of these informal gatherings represents something close to the freewheeling attitudes that characterized Village life.

27 UNION SQUARE WEST, STINSON RECORDS

Stinson Records began in 1939 as a distributor of Russian records in the United States. By 1943 Stinson went into partnership with Moe Asch's new record label, Asch Records. Asch thereby acquired distribution for his records, while Stinson was able to gain some income from the profits of Asch's recordings of Dylan's early hero Woody Guthrie. Under the name Asch-Stinson the labels produced records by such artists as Burl Ives, Josh White, and Lead Belly. In 1946 the labels split apart. In the 1950s, Bob Harris, son of the original co-owner Herbert Harris, operated a retail record store at their Union Square headquarters, and he continued to issue recordings by various folk singers, as well as a few world music artists and a few jazz musicians. Although the label did issue a few albums by younger Village folk artists, it basically became a reissue label.

41 WEST 16TH STREET

Joni Mitchell lived here in 1967, and wrote the song "Chelsea Morning" about the neighborhood.

GRAMERCY PARK EAST, 20TH–21ST STREETS BETWEEN PARK AVENUE SOUTH AND THIRD AVENUE

Gramercy Park is a two-acre private park, but the name is also used for the neighborhood the park is located in. Residents pay a fee to get the key to this quiet green space. The area is just north of Greenwich Village, but south of Midtown Manhattan. Dylan's manager Albert Grossman lived here before he moved to Woodstock. Bob Dylan would often visit and sometimes stayed there.

222 WEST 23RD STREET, CHELSEA HOTEL

29. Chelsea Hotel, ca. 1920s. New York Public Library Digital Collections.

The Chelsea boasted a mix of apartments and hotel rooms when Dylan lived in New York City. Although strictly speaking it is not located in the Village, its ambiance attracted such authors as Arthur Miller and Tennessee Williams, and beat novelist Jack Kerouac wrote his classic novel *On the Road* at the Chelsea. Dylan stayed here with his wife-to-be Sara for a period in 1964 (true fans will check out apartment 211), and some of the other musicians who stayed here were jazz composer and pianist Chick Corea, rock guitarist Jeff Beck, Patti Smith, the Grateful Dead, Janis Joplin, and Leonard Cohen. The permanent residents and the hotel's management have been embroiled in legal controversies for some 10 years, but the hotel began to gradually reopen in 2022.

10 WEST 28TH STREET, HOME OF EVE AND MAC MCKENZIE AND THEIR SON PETER MCKENZIE

During the spring and summer of 1961, Bob Dylan mostly resided at the home of the McKenzies. According to Peter McKenzie's book, he and Bob were so close that they were virtually brothers. Peter also seems to be the only person to whom Dylan actually taught guitar. Each morning the McKenzies would give Bob an "allowance" of fifty cents a day toward his expenses. Mac was an ex-official of the National Maritime Union who had been blacklisted during the McCarthy era. He was exceptionally well read and politically sophisticated. Eve was a former modern dancer who was very supportive of Bob's efforts. Both of them were enthusiastic folk fans, and Bob met such people as Woody Guthrie's close friend Cisco Houston, Harold Leventhal, manager of The Weavers, and Judy Collins through the McKenzies. The McKenzies recorded many of Dylan's early songs, and he even presented them with copies of his lyrics. He later gave permission to Peter to sell off some of these song lyric sheets when Eva was ill and badly in need of money.*

207 EAST 30TH STREET (BETWEEN SECOND AND THIRD AVENUES), COLUMBIA RECORDS STUDIOS

Nicknamed "The Church" because it was located in an old church building, Columbia's New York recording studio operated in this location from 1948 to 1981. (See

*See Peter McKenzie, *Bob Dylan: On a Couch & Fifty Cents a Day* (New York: MKB Press, 2021).

799 Seventh Avenue for their primary recording studios, where Dylan made his initial recordings.) Many classic albums, including Miles Davis's *Kind of Blue*, several original cast albums, and other albums by Columbia's classical and jazz roster, were recorded here through this period. Tom Wilson and Dylan worked on overdubbing electric instruments onto Dylan's earlier recording of "House of the Rising Sun" here after the Animals scored a pop hit with their cover version, but they ultimately abandoned the project. The building was demolished in 1985 and an apartment building is now located there.

Midtown

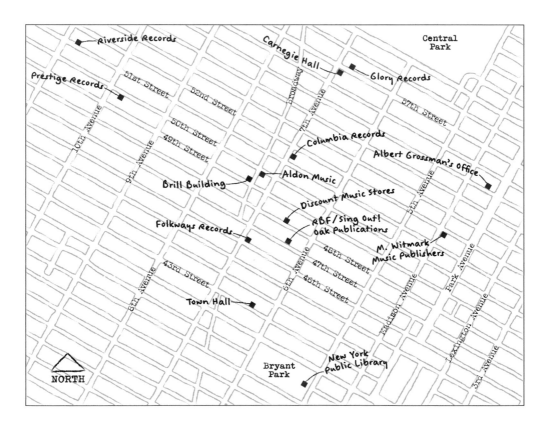

Although there were numerous performing venues in the Village and East Village, and several independent record labels were located there, the basic infrastructure of the music business was in Midtown Manhattan. Almost all the music publishing companies, record labels, recording studios, personal managers, and booking agents were located between 34th and 57th Streets between Lexington Avenue on the East and Eighth Avenue on the West.

FIFTH AVENUE BETWEEN 40TH AND 42ND STREETS, NEW YORK PUBLIC LIBRARY

In his early days in New York City, Bob spent many hours browsing at the huge main branch of the New York Public Library.

123 WEST 43RD STREET, TOWN HALL

Town Hall and Carnegie Hall have long and storied histories, and have featured thousands of performances of all kinds of music. On April 12, 1963, Bob Dylan performed his first solo concert at a major venue at Town Hall. It has seating capacity for 1,500 people.

165 WEST 46TH STREET, FOLKWAYS RECORDS
121 WEST 47TH STREET, RBF/*SING OUT!*/OAK PUBLICATIONS

Moses (Moe) Asch (1905–1986) was a unique character in the record industry. He went through two unsuccessful record companies, Asch and Disc, before establishing Folkways Records in 1948. Asch released over two thousand albums, helped sustain Pete Seeger's finances through the blacklist, and released albums produced by such musicians and scholars as John Cohen, Henry Cowell, and Mike Seeger, among many others. The six LPs in Harry Smith's *Anthology of American Folk Music* were devoured by Bob Dylan. Bob learned many of the songs, and used others as ingredients in some of his own creations.

Asch's original one-room office on 46th Street was divided into a small recording studio, which you entered directly as you opened the door, and on the other side a recording console and a desk. Later, Asch stopped recording there entirely and began using the studio operated by Mel Kaiser of Cue Recordings, which was located across the hall. Radio station WEVD, where Asch had previously worked in the '30s and early '40s, was also located in the building.

Asch was also involved in related businesses with his then-partner, Irwin Silber. A separate office was opened for this operation in the late '50s a block away on West 47th Street, which included Record, Book, and Film (RBF) sales (a direct mail operation to sell Folkways releases), *Sing Out!* magazine (the more-or-less official magazine of the folk movement), and Oak Publications (which published instruction and songbooks).*

Bob's original intention was to secure a recording contract with Folkways, so he set out to meet with Moe Asch. It is likely that he mistakenly went to the West 47th Street office, where Asch didn't actually work. He met instead with Irwin Silber, who dismissed the singer-songwriter, although later *Sing Out!* did print some of his songs. Silber wrote a scathing review of Dylan's performance at the 1965 Newport Folk Festival (where he "went electric"), reflecting the hardline, traditional viewpoint of the previous generation of folkies.

Oak Publications was sold to what became Music Sales Ltd. in the later 1960s, and *Sing Out!* was spun off as an independent company. After Asch's death, Folkways was acquired by the Smithsonian Institution, where it continues to release new and reissue albums today.

WEST 48TH STREET BETWEEN SIXTH AND SEVENTH AVENUES, DISCOUNT MUSIC STORES

The New York of the 1960s had entire blocks that specialized in particular merchandise. West 48th Street had an astounding collection of discount music stores. This included Terminal Music, Manny's, Sam Ash, Jimmy's, We Buy Guitars, and Noah Wolfe's. It was possible to go from one store to another in search of a particular item, and save a few dollars by pricing the item at all these stores. On Saturdays a pedestrian could witness suburban families in station wagons stopping at the stores and outfitting a complete band for their teenaged children. This might include guitars, trumpets, amplifiers, PA systems, and drum sets.

These were bustling enterprises, and many of the employees were semi-professional or professional musicians struggling to make a living. Dylan's friend Happy Traum taught guitar at Noah Wolfe's, the only one of the stores that offered lessons. Henry Goodrich of Manny's be-friended many musicians, and would cheerfully lend studio musicians instruments rent-free for recording sessions. Only Sam Ash has survived as a chain of music stores; all the rest were out of business due to rising

---

*For details about Smithsonian records, see Richard Carlin, *Worlds of Sound: The Story of Smithsonian Folkways* (Washington, DC: Smithsonian, 2008).

rents by 2015. Sam Ash and a few of the other stores moved to different locations in Manhattan.

MUSIC PUBLISHERS

Two midtown buildings housed the publishing companies and songwriters who wrote many of the rock-and-roll songs from 1950 to 1965. The Brill Building, located at 1619 Broadway (Broadway and 49th Street), was an eleven-story building that housed such hit songwriters as Burt Bacharach, Hal David and Doc Pomus, and Jerry Leiber and Mike Stoller. Up the street at 1650 Broadway, Donnie Kirchner and Al Nevins established Aldon Music. Among the hit writers who had writing cubicles in that building were Carole King and Gerry Goffin, Barry Mann and Cynthia Weill, and Jeff Barry and Ellie Greenwich. It was not unusual for these writers to write three songs a day, figuring that a small number of them would get recorded and an even smaller number would become hits. Bob Dylan turned this world on its ear. His lyrics were more adult and complex, and some of his songs were far longer than those of the Broadway songwriters.

446 WEST 50TH STREET, PRESTIGE RECORDS

Prestige, founded in 1949 by Bob Weinstock, was originally a label that specialized in modern jazz. In the mid-1950s, Prestige hired folklorist Ken Goldstein to produce folk records, and at the height of the folk revival launched Prestige Folklore and Prestige International labels for folk releases. Folklorist Sam Charters produced many of Prestige's folk material in the early to mid-1960s. Some of the people who recorded for Prestige were Geoff Muldaur, Tom Rush, and various blues artists. In 1971 the label was sold to Fantasy Records, and later to Concord.

553 WEST 51ST STREET, RIVERSIDE RECORDS

Like Prestige, Riverside was originally a jazz label. Kenneth Goldstein produced many folk music recordings for Riverside before he began working for Prestige. Some of the folk artists on Riverside were Oscar Brand, banjoist Billy Faier, Bob Gibson, and British folksinger and songwriter Ewan MacColl. In 1963 co-owner

Bill Grauer died of a heart attack, and the label ceased to operate a year later. Like Prestige, the company is now owned by large independent label Concord.

799 SEVENTH AVENUE, BETWEEN 51ST AND 52ND STREETS, COLUMBIA RECORDS

This was Columbia's other studio in New York where they recorded and mastered many of their pop releases (see also 207 East 30th Street). Dylan made his first recordings at the label's studio in this building as a harmonica player on Carolyn Hester's album that was recorded there in 1962, which was produced by John Hammond, who was impressed enough to later sign Bob to the label. Hester recalled that when she first met Dylan he "impressed me as being someone who probably never went outdoors . . . he's got that wonderful curly hair and white, white, ghostly white [skin]. I'm four years older, and I'm feeling a little worried about him, like a big sister."* Other artists who recorded there included Simon & Garfunkel and, later, Billy Joel. After Columbia shut down the studio in August 1966, it was sold to Phil Ramone, who opened his A&R Recording studio there. The entire building was demolished in 1985 to make way for the Equitable Building.

489 MADISON AVENUE (BETWEEN 51ST AND 52ND STREETS), M. WITMARK MUSIC PUBLISHERS

When John Hammond signed Bob Dylan to Columbia Records in 1962, he sent him over to veteran music publisher Lou Leeds. However, when manager Albert Grossman took over Dylan's affairs, he quickly arranged for Dylan's music to be published by M. Witmark. Dylan made some song demos there, which were later released by Columbia Records as part of their "bootleg" Bob Dylan album releases.

75 EAST 55TH STREET, ALBERT GROSSMAN'S OFFICE

Albert Grossman was possibly the first personal manager who fully grasped the importance of music publishing as an income stream for himself and for the

---

*Billy Heller, "How Bob Dylan Talked His Way into His First Recording Session 60 Years Ago," *New York Post*, November 17, 2021, nypost.com/2021/11/17/how-bob-dylan-landed-his-first-recording-session-60-years-ago/.

artists who he managed. Grossman built an empire around artists who were also songwriters, like Bob Dylan and Gordon Lightfoot. As their personal manager, he enjoyed income from their own recordings and performances, but also from artists like Peter, Paul and Mary (whom he also managed) or other artists who recognized the songwriting abilities of Dylan and Lightfoot. Grossman also brought on other lower-level managers like John Court and Charlie Rothschild, who worked with such Dylan clients as Odetta and Richie Havens.

157 WEST 57TH STREET, GLORY RECORDS

Glory Records was a small independent label that was important in the folk music revival because it released two hit folk-pop records. The first was "Cindy, Oh Cindy," recorded by Vince Martin backed by an early pop-folk group known as The Tarriers. This recording reached number 9 on the national pop charts. Six months later The Tarriers' recording of "The Banana Boat Song" reached number 4. These records were issued some four years after The Weavers had been blacklisted, and along with Harry Belafonte's recordings, they created new interest in American folk music.

Martin went on to perform and record with Village singer-songwriter Fred Neil. The original Tarriers included Alan Arkin, who went on to a successful acting career, Bob Carey, who continued to perform with the band, and Erik Darling, who replaced Pete Seeger in The Weavers and founded the folk-rock band The Rooftop Singers.

881 SEVENTH AVENUE AT 57TH STREET, CARNEGIE HALL

Carnegie Hall opened in 1891. The main hall has a seating capacity of 2,804, and there are also two smaller halls in the building. On October 26, 1963, Bob Dylan performed at Carnegie Hall for the first time.

8

South and East of Washington Square Park/ The Lower East Side

Although the Lower East Side is not geographically part of Greenwich Village, the availability of low-cost rental housing led to the opening of jazz clubs, artists' lofts, and theaters. In the Village itself Irish and Italians were the dominant residents, but on the Lower East Side the demographic mix included a large Eastern European Jewish population as well as other Eastern Europeans, Italians, Puerto Ricans, and African Americans. As is the case with Greenwich Village, the gentrification of the neighborhood has resulted in a wealthier and less ethnically heterogeneous group of residents.

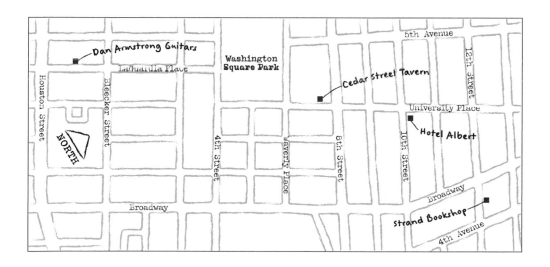

24 UNIVERSITY PLACE, CEDAR STREET TAVERN

The Cedar Street Tavern was particularly known as a gathering place for visual artists. Many of the lions of American impressionistic art drank there. This included chronic drunken misbehaving Jackson Pollock, Franz Kline, Willem de Kooning, and younger colleague Larry Rivers. Composers Morton Feldman and John Cage, playwright and poet LeRoi Jones (Amiri Baraka), poet Allen Ginsberg, and art critic Clement Greenberg were also frequent visitors. The atmosphere was charged with an argumentative spirit, and beat novelist Jack Kerouac and Jackson Pollock were both kicked out of the Cedar for misbehavior. When the Cedar moved to 82 University in 1962 the artists did not move with it, but chose to patronize bars in the East Village. Around March, 1965, Bob Dylan and his friend Bobby Neuwirth met there with D.A. Pennebaker to discuss the Dylan documentary film that became *Don't Look Back*.

500 LAGUARDIA PLACE, DAN ARMSTRONG GUITARS

In the early 1960s, Dan Armstrong moved to New York City from his hometown of Pittsburgh. He wanted to work as a studio musician and guitar repair man. Dan opened a repair shop at Seventh Avenue and 49th Street in 1965. This was a block away from a string of music stores on 48th Street, and soon Dan was doing repairs for the many studio guitarists who were playing on recording sessions. Because the store was located so close to the midtown recording studios where these musicians worked, they could bring in guitars for quick readjustments and then continue to play their next recording sessions. It was not unusual to witness studio musicians jamming and exchanging ideas about guitars or guitar music while Dan was working on their instruments. Dan also loved to play guitar, and in 1967 he played in Van Morrison's road band with guitarist Charlie Brown, who was a session musician at Atlantic records, and later was a member of Eric Weissberg's band Deliverance.

In 1968 the building Dan's shop was in was torn down, and Dan moved to 500 LaGuardia Place, just south of Bleecker Street. He was then hired as a consultant by the Ampeg Company, and he designed a line of guitars and electric basses that were made of plexiglass. In the early '70s Armstrong moved to London, where he developed a new line of instruments, amplifiers, and effects boxes. From the '70s until his death in 2004, Armstrong lived variously in London and the United States. Some of his employees became well known in their own rights. Eddie Diehl was a jazz guitarist who became known for his neck repair work for Armstrong, and another employee, Carl Thompson makes electric basses.

40 KENMARE STREET, JOHN D'ANGELICO GUITARS

John D'Angelico apprenticed with his uncle, Raphael Ciani, who taught him how to build violins, mandolins, and guitars. Originally, he had fifteen employees, but he preferred to devote his efforts to building instruments, not managing employees. Consequently, he opened his own small shop at 40 Kenmare Street in 1932 with two employees. D'Angelico built over eleven hundred guitars, mostly f-hole archtops, along with a handful of round-hole guitars and mandolins. Many of the working guitarists who were studio musicians owned D'Angelico Guitars. In 1952 Jimmy D'Aquisto joined the company as an apprentice. After John's death, D'Aquisto bought the shop from the family, eventually moving it to Long Island. Like D'Angelico, D'Aquisto became a legendary figure among guitar players, with his guitars becoming collectible and expensive items.

Guitar repair specialists have a long and often well-deserved reputation for being somewhat lax about completing work on time. Several years ago, I had acquired a banjo from a pawn shop in Philadelphia, and following the directions in Pete Seeger's instruction book, I took it to D'Angelico's shop to have him extend the neck of the instrument by three frets. D'Angelico gave me a date when the job would be done, and I took the train from Philadelphia, only to find that he had not even begun to work on the instrument. I made the same trip the second time, with a similar result. When I arrived at the shop for the third time, John took pity on me, told me to have lunch and come back. Sure enough, he had completed the job while I was eating lunch.

BOB DYLAN, RADIO, AND OSCAR BRAND

Bob Dylan's first radio appearance was on the Oscar Brand's WNYC radio show, *Folksong Festival*, on October 29, 1961, to help promote his Carnegie Chapter Hall performance promoted by Israel Young, owner of the Folklore Center. Brand (1920–2016) holds the Guinness record for longevity of a radio host of a single show: *Oscar Brand's Folksong Festival* ran from 1945 to 2015. Cynthia Gooding was also a singer and radio personality who featured Dylan on several of her

30. Woody Guthrie and Oscar Brand, ca. late 1950s. Photo Sound Associates. From the Ronald D. Cohen Collection #20239, Southern Folklife Collection, The Wilson Library, University of North Carolina at Chapel Hill.

shows. Brand's show, however, had a particular cachet, based upon his hyperactive performing and recording career.

Brand himself lived in the Village after serving in World War II. A non-communist liberal, Brand was nevertheless blacklisted because he often had guest artists who were deemed to be left-wing subversives by Red Channels and other blacklisting sources. His career including writing the lyrics to Doris Day's hit song "A Guy Is a Guy," over one hundred albums, and countless performances. Since Brand was a native Canadian, his resourceful answer to the blacklist was to host a Canadian TV show from 1963 to 1967. He also wrote seven books and produced numerous television shows and authored several theatrical works.

Cooper Square

In the 1960s, two important buildings dominated Cooper Square. Carl Fischer Music, at 62 Cooper Square, was the home of music publisher Carl Fischer. The building included a large retail sheet music store and a printing facility that printed the company's music. Millions of copies of sheet music were distributed around the world. Carl Fischer published the music of John Philip Sousa, Fritz Kreisler, Sergei Rachmaninoff, and Ernest Bloch, among others. In 1999 the company moved its headquarters to Wall Street, and abandoned the retail store. The space is now occupied by condominiums.

THE COOPER UNION

Investor, industrialist, and philanthropist Peter Cooper established The Cooper Union for the Advancement of Science and Art in 1859. The school specializes in art, architecture, and engineering. For many years it offered free tuition, but its 2012 decision to begin charging tuition created a thunderstorm of protest. Currently the trustees hope to restore free tuition by 2029. In addition to the school, which has an international reputation, the facility boasts a 900-seat Great Hall. Speakers at the hall have included Abraham Lincoln, Lakota Sioux chief Red Cloud, women's rights agitator Susan B. Anthony, Mark Twain, and Barack Obama.

The Lower East Side (The East Village)

The area east of Broadway and running to the East River was originally known as the Lower East Side. As real estate prices in Greenwich Village escalated developers chose to cast this area in a new light by referring to it as the "East Village." The East Village had a somewhat different population base than its western cousin, including Ukrainians, Eastern Europeans, Italians, and Russian Jews. In the western part of the East Village, the Bowery ran from Third Avenue and Fourth Street to downtown, well south of Greenwich Village. It was noted for cheap artist studios, flophouses for the indigent, and numerous drinking establishments.

A unique feature of the area was the four dozen bookshops that extended down Fourth Avenue from Union Square to Astor Place on Fourth Avenue. These bookstores began to go under starting in the depression of the 1930s, and continuing with extensive rent increases in the 1950s. By the 1960s only the Strand Bookshop remained. In 1996 a small used bookstore called the Alabaster Bookshop opened across the street from the relocated Strand, at Broadway and 12th Street.

BROADSIDE MAGAZINE

Two of the original members of the Almanac Singers, Gordon Friesen and Sis Cunningham, became frustrated when *Sing Out!* magazine increasingly turned away from its focus on songs of social protest. With some financial aid from folk singer Pete Seeger, they set out to remedy that situation by publishing a mimeographed magazine of topical songs called *Broadside* in 1962. The magazine was originally headquartered in their apartment on the Lower East Side. Folk singer Gil Turner brought Dylan into the fold, and, along with numerous other folk singers including Phil Ochs, Len Chandler, and Tom Paxton, he attended monthly meetings and submitted songs to the magazine. According to Friesen and Cunningham, Dylan came to the meetings for a year before turning toward more personal and surrealistic songs. In 1964 the couple moved uptown to 215 West 98th Street, and by 1988 the magazine had folded, but Folkways Records issued many of the songs that had been tape recorded at the Broadside apartment.*

23 EAST 10TH STREET, HOTEL ALBERT

Like the Earle (see 103 Waverly Place), the Hotel Albert was an inexpensive, somewhat dingy hotel that was favored by many of the musicians who worked or were performing in the Village. It was somewhat east of the various performing spaces in the Village, in a quieter neighborhood.

In 1875–1876 two houses were converted into a building that contained twenty-four apartments, but in 1887 the space was made into a hotel. Over the next 20 years an additional story was added to the building, and the property was subdivided into the Albert and a property leased for commercial usage. The original guests included numerous artists, including authors Robert Louis Stephenson and Thomas Wolfe, and poets Walt Whitman and Hart Crane. The hotel also had a radical political history; John Thomas Scopes, the subject of the famous 1925 Monkey Trail, stayed here, and the Communist Party held secret meetings in the Albert basement

---

*For many details about Broadside and their lives in the radical song movement, see Agnes "Sis" Cunningham and Gordon Friesen, *Red Dust and Broadsides: A Joint Autobiography* (Amherst: University of Massachusetts Press, 1999).

during the McCarthy period of the 1950s. Anaïs Nin (1903–1977) said that at this time the hotel was "full of students, all-night saxophones, bathroom down the hall."*

By the mid-'60s such folk-rock luminaries as the Mamas & the Papas and the Lovin' Spoonful stayed at the hotel. The Spoonful even had a rehearsal space in the basement, and lead singer John Sebastian wrote their first hit song, "Do You Believe in Magic," there. John and Michelle Phillips wrote the first hit for the Mamas & the Papas, "California Dreaming," either at the Albert or at the Earle, where they also sometimes stayed. In 1984 real estate developers turned the Albert into 190 co-op apartments.

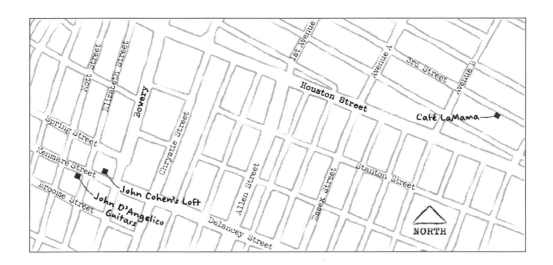

BLEECKER BETWEEN ELIZABETH STREET AND THE BOWERY, JOHN COHEN'S LOFT

The late John Cohen was a photographer and musician. He was one of the founding members of the New Lost City Ramblers, a folk music revival band that focused on mountain music from the Southern Appalachians. Cohen was a dedicated purist who scorned commercial pop-folk music, but he became fascinated by Bob Dylan. Dylan asked Cohen to take some of his publicity photos, which Cohen

---

*Quoted in "A Brief History," *Hotel Albert*, 2011, thehotelalbert.com/history.html.

31. John Cohen in his loft, ca. 1960. Photo: Sound Associates. From the Ronald D. Cohen Collection #20239, Southern Folklife Collection, The Wilson Library, University of North Carolina at Chapel Hill.

took on the roof and the street around his loft. Cohen helped promote Dylan in his early years in folk music journals and later published the book *Young Bob: John Cohen's Early Photographs of Bob Dylan*. In Dylan's book *Chronicles*, he describes seeing fellow Rambler Mike Seeger playing at Alan Lomax's loft and coming to the realization that he would never approach Seeger's instrumental virtuosity but could make his own contribution to the folk revival through his songwriting gifts.

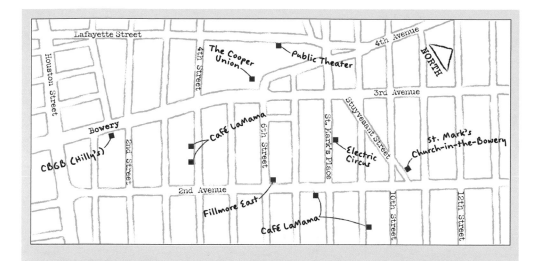

THEATER IN THE EAST VILLAGE

The East Village was truly a hotbed of theater, starting in the 1960s. Ralph Cook's Theater Genesis was housed at St. Mark's Church-in-the-Bowery, at Second Avenue and East 10th Street. Cook was a strong civil rights activist who was hired by the church in 1964. He then launched the theater, which was focused on the street life of ordinary people. His intent was to help refine plays that were in an early process of development. He left the theater in 1969, and it closed a few years later.

JULIAN BECK AND JUDITH MALINA: THE LIVING THEATRE

Julian Beck (1925–1985) and Judith Malina (1926–2015) founded the Living Theater in 1947. During the 1950s they produced works by influential European playwrights ranging from Bertold Brecht to Pablo Picasso and Luigi Pirandello. They had continual conflicts with the city over tax disputes and were even briefly imprisoned. Their original space was at Third Street and Avenue C; it closed in 1993. They continued their activities in Europe and then at 19–21 Clinton Street. That space closed in 2013, and today the theater has resumed its nomadic ways, with no set space for its offerings.

The Living Theater is the oldest experimental theater company in the United States. Because of its anarchist political ideology and its non-commercial orientation, it is generally regarded as being one of the founders of the off-off Broadway theater.

ELLEN STEWART AND LA MAMA

Ellen Stewart (1919–2011) was not an actress, a director, or a producer, yet she was a vital force in off-off-Broadway theater. Stewart worked in the fashion industry at Saks Fifth Avenue for some 30 years. She founded Café La MaMa in 1961 to give her foster brother an opportunity to get his work produced. Her theater nurtured playwrights Sam Shepherd, Lanford Wilson, and Harvey Fierstein, as well as actors Al Pacino, Robert De Niro, and Bette Midler. The theater moved to various spaces in the East Village, including 321 East Ninth Street, 122 Second Avenue, 74 East Fourth Street, 236 East Third Street, and 66 East Fourth Street. Late in her career Stewart even directed several shows herself. She taught in many nations and she also produced dozens of plays by foreign authors at her theater.

Stewart constantly battled city inspectors seeking code violations, and the neighbors in the building housing the theater accused her of running a house of prostitution. A health inspector then advised her to get a coffeehouse license rather than a theatrical one, explaining that it was easier to get a license to serve coffee than to operate a theater.

JOSEPH PAPP: THE PUBLIC THEATER

Joseph Papp (1921–1991) followed a very different path than Beck, Malina, or Stewart. He presented free city-sponsored Shakespeare productions in midtown's Central Park, but he also presented the work of young playwrights in The Public Theater at 425 Lafayette Street. The building contains five different theater spaces.

Papp seemed to have a special talent for recognizing off-Broadway works that could be moved to Broadway for long and successful runs that greatly aided the finances of his theater. Examples include *Hair* and *A Chorus Line*. The tradition continued after Papp's death with the production of Lin-Manuel Miranda's *Hamilton* in 2015.

SIXTH STREET AND SECOND AVENUE, FILLMORE EAST

The Fillmore East was an east-coast outlet for promoter-entrepreneur Bill Graham, whose Fillmore West in San Francisco was a widely celebrated rock venue. The Fillmore East operated from 1968 to 1971, and featured an eclectic line-up that focused on rock acts, but spilled over into jazz and other musical genres. The music was

32. Fillmore East building. Photo: GVSHP. Creative Commons BY 2.0 license.

accompanied by the Joshua Light Show, and Graham often employed mixed musical bills that featured artists whose music fit into wildly differing musical styles. I recall attending one such show where jazz trumpet player Miles Davis opened for singer-songwriter-rocker Neil Young. Jimi Hendrix and the Grateful Dead were among the artists who played the Fillmore East, and many live recordings were made there.

313–315 BOWERY, CBGB (HILLY'S)

Although the club's name stood for Country, Bluegrass, and Blues, it was best known for featuring such punk and new wave groups as the Ramones, Blondie, and Talking Heads. Before owner Hilly Kristol opened his club, it was an infamous flophouse. The club closed in 2006, and the current tenants include a clothing boutique and a fine art photography gallery.

19–25 ST. MARKS PLACE, ELECTRIC CIRCUS

The building that housed the Circus had a rich and colorful history. It was a German music society clubhouse in the 1870s, and then a ballroom and community hall.

It later witnessed a shootout between rival Italian American and Jewish American gangsters, and it housed a Polish restaurant and meeting place for Polish organizations. The Polish organization became the Dom Restaurant and then in 1966 artist Andy Warhol and film director Paul Morrisey rented it for their "happening," "The Exploding Plastic Inevitable," which featured the Velvet Underground and various Warhol "superstars." They performed with many effects such as projected movies and photographs and light show effects.

In 1966 Albert Grossman, Bob Dylan's manager, tried to turn the club into the Balloon Farm, but he gave up the lease a year later. From 1967 until 1971 it became the nightclub the Electric Circus. There were light shows, jugglers, and trapeze artists. The bands were a diverse lot, including the Grateful Dead, Ike and Tina Turner, electronic music pioneer Morton Subotnick, the Allman Brothers, and Sly & the Family Stone. In 1970 a bomb was set off in the club, and this hastened its decline. The space is currently an upscale apartment and retail space.

9

By the Time He Got to Woodstock

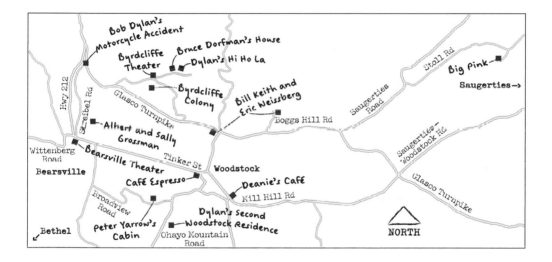

Woodstock is a very small town located not quite one hundred and ten miles north and slightly west of New York City. Many large cities in the United States similarly have some sort of small-town arts-oriented community that serves as a weekend refuge or vacation spot for tranquility-seeking urban residents where they can get away to a world that is more oriented toward natural beauty rather than urban development. These include New Hope, Pennsylvania, for Philadelphia; Lenox, Nantucket, and Martha's Vineyard, Massachusetts, for Boston; Sedona, Arizona, for Phoenix; and Cannon Beach, Oregon, for Portland.

Mapping the Territory

Here are a few key locations that relate to Bob Dylan's Woodstock years. Clustered within a couple of miles or so are the locations of Bob Dylan's first and second houses, and the homes of his various friends and business associates.

BROADVIEW ROAD, PETER YARROW'S CABIN

Peter Yarrow, the Peter of Peter, Paul and Mary, had been coming to Woodstock since the mid-1940s. His family owned two cabins there and used them as a summer hideaway from the heat of New York City. Yarrow recalled inviting Dylan to visit him in town just before the famous March on Washington:

> I invited Bob Dylan and Suze, his girlfriend, to come up and stay with me. My mother was there, and they went and stayed at Twin Gables. Suze and I went to Art Students league, and Bob would be writing songs like Only A Pawn In Their Game, and Bob Dylan's Dream. . . . It was an extraordinary time . . . an idyllic time.*

By 1963, Albert Grossman, who managed both Peter, Paul and Mary and Bob Dylan, moved to Bearsville, close to Woodstock, and Dylan was introduced to Woodstock through visits with both Yarrow and Grossman. Dylan then bought his first Woodstock house in the former Byrdcliffe Colony.

Grossman proceeded to build a recording studio, and he acquired various properties in town. Within the next five years a substantial number of musicians moved to town, and essentially created their own community within the town.

59 TINKER STREET, CAFÉ ESPRESSO

Tinker Street is the downtown commercial hub of Woodstock. In 1959 Bernard and Mary Lou Paturel bought a former ice cream parlor called the Nook and trans-

---

*Heylin, *The Double Life of Bob Dylan*, 207; also quoted in Brian Hollander, "Peter Yarrow Returns to Woodstock," *Hudson Valley One*, June 8, 2018, hudsonvalleyone.com/2018/06/08/peter-yarrow-returns-to-woodstock/.

33. Happy Traum, ca. 1960. Photo: Sound Associates. From the Ronald D. Cohen Collection #20239, Southern Folklife Collection, The Wilson Library, University of North Carolina at Chapel Hill.

formed it into the Café Espresso. During his early Woodstock years, Dylan became friendly with them, and they allowed him the rent-free use of an upstairs space, where he kept a typewriter and wrote songs. Dylan dominated the checkerboard at the establishment. The Center for Photography now occupies the site.

Guitarist Happy Traum recalls his first trip to Woodstock to play at the Café:

I took the bus from New York City and was picked up by the proprietor, Bernard Paturel, French and suave with his brushed mustaches and vaguely Gallic accent. He took me to his apartment above the club to meet Marylou and their small children, and then down to the Cafe, which was warm and cozy after the long, snowy bus ride. The room was already crowded with local folk who had come more to get out of the cold than to see a young unknown folksinger from the city, but everyone was as welcoming as the room itself.*

18 STREIBEL ROAD, BEARSVILLE, HOME OF ALBERT AND SALLY GROSSMAN

Bearsville is just west of Woodstock. It was here that Albert Grossman settled and built his empire, which included his home and his Bearsville Recording Studios. Dylan met his wife Sara through her friendship with Sally Grossman. Grossman is buried in the woods nearby.

109 MILL HILL ROAD, DEANIE'S CAFÉ

A burger-and-brew joint favored as a late-night hang by Dylan, The Band, Van Morrison, and other musicians. The site is now the home of the restaurant Cucina Woodstock.

2277 GLASCO TURNPIKE AND 60 BOGGS HILL ROAD, HOMES OF BILL KEITH AND ERIC WEISSBERG

Banjo pioneers Bill Keith and Eric Weissberg lived just down the road from one another in Woodstock. Keith was one of the inventors of the post–Earl Scruggs melodic banjo style, and Weissberg was known for the *Deliverance* movie score and his hit recording of the song "Dueling Banjos." Eric also played on the original sessions for Dylan's 1975 album, *Blood On The Tracks*.

---

*Happy Traum, "Music from Home—A Life in Woodstock, NY," *Happy Traum* (blog), accessed June 7, 2022, www.happytraum.com/post/music-from-home-a-life-in-woodstock-ny.

34. Eric Weissberg playing the banjo in Washington Square Park. Photo: Sound Associates. From the Ronald D. Cohen Collection #20239, Southern Folklife Collection, The Wilson Library, University of North Carolina at Chapel Hill.

GLASCO TURNPIKE AND STREIBEL ROAD,
BOB DYLAN'S MOTORCYCLE ACCIDENT

This is the site of Bob Dylan's motorcycle accident in 1966. This accident effectively ended the first phrase of Dylan's career as a touring artist, and allowed Bob and The Band time to develop their song collaborations and recordings.

380 UPPER BYRDCLIFFE ROAD, BYRDCLIFFE THEATER

The town of Woodstock dates from the late eighteenth century. By the late 1800s, several visual artists had flocked to Woodstock and established what was known as the Byrdcliffe Colony. In 1916 a music chapel was built in the woods to host Maverick Concerts, an annual chamber music festival that often features premiere performances of new works. It is the longest-running summer chamber music festival in the United States.

CAMELOT ROAD, BOB DYLAN'S FIRST WOODSTOCK HOME, KNOWN AS HI LO HA

Dylan moved into this home in summer 1965. Although local residents mostly allowed Bob to have his own space, as his popularity increased, several unwanted visitors would appear in town, or on or near his property. By 1968 Bob had put his house up for sale, and he and Sara moved to their second Woodstock residence in 1969.

CAMELOT ROAD, BRUCE DORFMAN'S HOUSE

Woodstock visual artist Bruce Dorfman lived next door to Dylan. They would frequently encounter one another as they walked their kids to the school bus stop. After Dylan's motorcycle accident, Dylan took painting lessons from Dorfman. When Bob returned to New York City he took further art lessons from painter Norman Raeben in 1974.

ALBERT GROSSMAN AND ARTIE TRAUM

Many musicians either followed Bob Dylan to Woodstock from New York City, or came due to the influence of these people. A few musicians, including dobro player Cindy Cashdollar, banjoist Billy Faier, and folklorist Sam Eskin, were long-time residents in the town years before Dylan moved there. Others were influenced by Albert Grossman and the various business enterprises that he pursued. Many of the musicians who moved to town, like Happy Traum and his younger brother Artie and bluegrass singer-guitarist Johnny Herald, knew Dylan from his

35. Happy and Artie Traum at the Bitter End, 1969. Photo: Diana Jo Davies. Ralph Rinzler Folklife Archives and Collections, Diana Davies Collection, Smithsonian Center for Folklife and Cultural Heritage.

early Greenwich Village days. Other Woodstock émigrés were Geoff and Maria (D'Amato) Muldaur, veterans of the New York and Boston jug band scene. Periodically Dylan would participate in jam sessions with these old friends.

In 1968 I was visiting Artie Traum, who was babysitting at Dylan's Hi Lo Ha house while it was up for sale. Artie was living rent-free in the house in exchange for making sure that no one vandalized the property. One day Albert Grossman called Artie and suggested that since he was living rent-free, he might consider paying the heating bill. Artie responded that the bill for heating this large house during the cold Woodstock winters would be double the cost of renting his own place. Albert never brought the subject up again. It was as though Grossman simply could not allow any financial opportunity to pass him by. Artie took me into an empty room that was almost entirely covered with sacks full of mail that no one had ever opened. We both quickly became aware of just how influential Bob Dylan had become.

36. Bearsville Theater. Photo: Paul Comstock. Creative Commons BY 2.0 license.

TINKER STREET AND WITTENBERG ROAD,
THE BEAR, LITTLE BEAR, AND BEARSVILLE THEATER

Albert Grossman became something of a real estate mogul in and around Woodstock. He owned the Bearsville Recording Studios, which included a record label, as well as the Bearsville Theater, a restaurant, and a saloon. The properties were situated on fifteen acres of land that Grossman owned.

OHAYO MOUNTAIN ROAD, DYLAN'S
SECOND WOODSTOCK RESIDENCE

In 1969 Dylan moved a few miles south of the Hi Lo Ha residence to a more iso-lated home located on Ohayo Mountain Road. Although this house had gates and fences, Dylan discovered that this was more of a challenge to Dylan-seekers rather than an impediment to their ability to find him. By the end of the year the Dylans had purchased their town house on MacDougal Street and left Woodstock.

WOODSTOCK'S JAZZ SCENE

Woodstock developed an intense experimental jazz scene shortly after Dylan left town. Under the leadership of Karl Berger, the Creative Music Studio established multiple residences, played and recorded hundreds of concerts, and taught many students who developed important careers of their own. Among them are guitarist Peter Bernstein and pianist Marilyn Crispell. Although the studio no longer has a permanent facility, it continues to hold classes and present concerts in rented spaces. Pianist-composer Carla Bley and her husband and bass player, Steve Swallow, live a few miles from Woodstock, and the late Burrill Crohn, a film and TV director, produced several films documenting various aspects of jazz history from 1978 to 2013.

56 PARNASSUS LANE, SAUGERTIES, BIG PINK

After Bob's motorcycle accident, he invited The Band to come to Woodstock to help him write and record songs. Band lead guitarist Robbie Robertson and his

37. Big Pink, home of the Band. Photo: John Dan. Creative Commons Attribution 2.0 Generic license.

wife moved next door to Albert Grossman, who managed The Band and procured a recording contract for them on Capitol Records. The rest of The Band members lived east of Woodstock in the town of Saugerties, in a fabled house that became known as Big Pink, where they rehearsed, recorded, and sometimes wrote songs with Dylan. Robertson recalled, "This ugly pink house became our clubhouse. It felt like what the Dead End Kids would have in the city, or the Bowery Boys—a place to go every day and hang around." The famous Basement Tapes were recorded there.*

LEAVING WOODSTOCK

Bob Dylan had other reasons for leaving Woodstock besides a loss of privacy. By 1968 he had begun separating himself from his manager Albert Grossman. The financial disagreements between the two ended in lengthy lawsuits that were not resolved until after Grossman's death in 1986. It is questionable that Dylan could have anticipated the importance of the 1969 Woodstock Festival. Although it was actually held in Bethel, some fifty-eight miles southwest of Woodstock, it went down in history as the Woodstock Festival, generating a whole huge crop of tourists and music fans looking to contact Dylan, who did not attend or play at the shindig. The Dylan family's return to New York City fits comfortably under the title of Thomas Wolfe's novel, *You Can't Go Home Again*. It is difficult to imagine that Dylan could have even harbored a suspicion that he was trading life in the country for the relentless stalking of A. J. Weberman.

---

*Jason Fine, "Summer of Love: Woodstock," *Rolling Stone*, December 11, 2007, www.rolling stone.com/music/music-news/summer-of-love-woodstock-75984/.

10

Other Famous Village Inhabitants

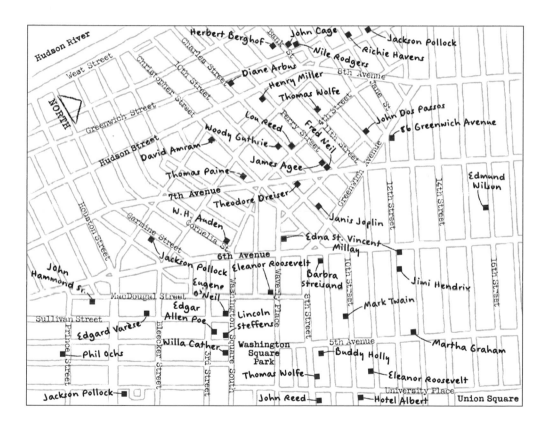

Over the years, artists, writers, musicians, and dancers have been a vaunted feature of Greenwich Village life. This chapter lists some of these luminaries. The reader should understand that the people listed stayed in the Village for varying amounts of time, and in some cases moved frequently from one address to another. When the person listed is deceased, I have included their birth and death dates.

JAMES AGEE, 38 PERRY STREET

Agee (1909–1955) was a poet, novelist, film critic, and screenwriter.

DAVID AMRAM, 114 CHRISTOPHER STREET; PRIOR TO THAT, EIGHTH STREET BETWEEN AVENUES B AND C

Amram is a nonagenarian composer and French horn player who has retained a lifelong interest in almost every genre of music. He and Bob Dylan met at the Eighth Street Bookshop in 1964, and the two recorded as accompanists to poet Allen Ginsberg in the late '60s and early '70s.

DIANE ARBUS, 121½ CHARLES STREET

Arbus (1923–1971) was a wide-ranging photographer whose subjects ranged from strippers to middle-class families and elderly subjects.

W.H. AUDEN, 7 CORNELIA STREET

Auden (1907–1993) was a famous poet. He was born in England, but moved to the United States and became an American citizen. Some critics believe that Dylan's 1967 song "As I Went Out One Morning" was influenced by Auden's poem "As I Went Out One Evening."

HERBERT BERGHOF STUDIO, 120 BANK STREET

Berghof (1909–1990) and his wife, Uta Hagen (1919–2004), taught acting at their studio for many years. A few of their many distinguished alumni include Anne Bancroft, Jeff Bridges, Billy Crystal, Bette Midler, and Hal Holbrook.

JOHN CAGE, 107 BANK STREET

Cage (1912–1992) was an avant-garde composer and music theorist. One of his best-known pieces, *4'33"*, consists entirely of silence as a pianist sits down to the keyboard, rustles around and changes position, never playing a single note.

WILLA CATHER, 60 WASHINGTON SQUARE SOUTH

Cather (1873–1947) was a well-known novelist of the late nineteenth and early twentieth century.

JOHN DOS PASSOS, 11 BANK STREET

Dos Passos (1896–1970) is best known for his ground-breaking *U.S.A.* trilogy of novels. He was originally a left-leaning activist, but as he became older his political views turned conservative.

THEODORE DREISER, 165 WEST 10TH STREET

Dreiser's (1871–1945) *Sister Carrie* and *An American Tragedy* were considered major works in the early twentieth century, but his reputation is somewhat in decline.

MARTHA GRAHAM, 66 FIFTH AVENUE

Graham (1894–1991) was one of the most significant figures in modern dance as a dancer, choreographer, and teacher.

WOODY GUTHRIE, 74 CHARLES STREET

Woody (1912–1967) was a major influence on Bob Dylan. He wrote hundreds of songs, and was a member of the Almanac Singers. He also was a strong influence on Pete Seeger.

JOHN HAMMOND SR., A CONDO ON MACDOUGAL BELOW HOUSTON STREET

John Hammond (1910–1987) signed Bob Dylan to Columbia Records, and was known as a man with an ear for talent. Among the musicians whose careers he influenced were Charley Christian, Billie Holiday, Bruce Springsteen, and Stevie Ray Vaughan.

RICHIE HAVENS, 61 JANE STREET

38. Richie Havens at Newport, 1965. Photo: Diana Jo Davies. Ralph Rinzler Folklife Archives and Collections, Diana Davies Collection, Smithsonian Center for Folklife and Cultural Heritage.

Richie Havens (1941–2013) began his career as a portrait artist in the Village. Partnering with a frame shop, he did his portraits in various parts of the Village. He developed an interest in the guitar while hanging out on clubs. His career caught fire at the Woodstock festival, when his set was extended because the next performer had not yet arrived. With his soulful singing, Richie was an outstanding interpreter of Dylan songs, especially "All Along the Watchtower."

JIMI HENDRIX, 59 WEST 12TH STREET

Famed rock artist Hendrix (1942–1970) lived here at the end of his life, while he was working on his Electric Lady recording studio. Dylan and Hendrix were said to have met only once, at the Kettle of Fish.

BUDDY HOLLY, 11 FIFTH AVENUE

The early rock-and-roll songwriter and performer lived here in the late 1950s. Dylan claimed to have been in the audience when Holly performed in Duluth on his fateful last tour.

JANE JACOBS, 555 HUDSON STREET

Jacobs (1916–2006) was influential in defending existing neighborhoods from the encroachment of developers, and for her books about creating livable cities.

JANIS JOPLIN, 139 WEST 10TH STREET

Joplin (1943–1970) lived here shortly before her death. She was a renowned blues-rock singer. She was managed by Al Grossman, who also managed Bob Dylan. When she was first living in San Francisco, Joplin met Dylan at a local club. "Bob, I just love you," she said. "I'm gonna be famous some day." Dylan replied, "Yeah, we're all gonna be famous."[*]

EDNA ST. VINCENT MILLAY, 139 WAVERLY PLACE, LATER 77 WEST 12TH STREET

Two of several Village homes of the poet and playwright Millay (1892–1950).

---

*Bill DeMain, "The Hard and Fast Times of Janis Joplin," *Louder*, May 13, 2016, www.loudersound.com/features/janis-joplin-little-girl-blue.

HENRY MILLER, 106 PERRY STREET

Miller (1891–1980) was an innovative novelist with a no-holds-barred approach to sex, resulting in several obscenity trials concerning his novels.

FRED NEIL, 32 PERRY STREET

Fred Neil (1936–2001) was a singer-songwriter who was performing at the Café Wha? when Dylan hit town; Dylan made his first appearance there playing harmonica with Neil. Never as successful as critics had wished him to be, Fred is remembered for his song "Everybody's Talkin'," performed by Harry Nilsson in the movie *Midnight Cowboy*. Neil devoted the last part of his life to protecting and conserving dolphins.

PHIL OCHS, 156 PRINCE STREET

Ochs (1940–1976) was a protest singer and a contemporary of Bob Dylan. Ochs recorded several albums, and some of his songs were covered by more famous artists. Most of his songs concerned social and political issues. Ochs idolized Dylan's work, but suffered personal rejection at his hands.

EUGENE O'NEILL, 38 WASHINGTON SQUARE SOUTH

O'Neill (1888–1953) was one of the most important playwrights of the first half of the twentieth century.

THOMAS (TOM) PAINE, 59 GROVE STREET

Paine (1737–1809) was one of the founding fathers of the American republic. His voice was an important one in the Revolutionary War period.

EDGAR ALLAN POE, 85 WEST 3RD STREET

Poe (1862–1910) was a poet, short story writer, and literary critic. Renowned as a mystery writer, his name is honored with an annual mystery writers' award. In his 2020 song "I Contain Multitudes," Dylan compares himself to Poe.

JACKSON POLLOCK, 47 HORATIO STREET, 46 CARMINE STREET, AND 76 WEST HOUSTON STREET

Pollock (1912–1956) was an important abstract expressionist artist who explored the technique of dripping paintings rather than using conventional brush painting techniques.

JOHN REED, 46 EAST EIGHTH STREET

Reed (1887–1920) is best known for his account of the Russian Revolution, *Ten Days That Shook the World*. In 1982 Warren Beatty produced and starred in the movie *Reds*, which was a biography of Reed.

LOU REED, 53 CHARLES STREET

Reed (1942–2013) was the principal songwriter and a founding member for the rock band the Velvet Underground. His widow, Laurie Anderson, is a well-respected experimental music composer and performer.

NILE RODGERS, 780 GREENWICH STREET

Rodgers was a versatile studio guitarist, and co-founder with bass player Bernard Edwards of the successful disco band Chic. Rodgers only worked with Dylan once, producing a version of "Ring of Fire" for the soundtrack to the film *Feeling Minnesota*. As Rodgers recalled,

> "At the time, the Unabomber hadn't been captured yet, but there was that artist rendering of him everywhere. Bob Dylan used to dress like the Unabomber. When he came to my apartment, my doorman freaked out and wouldn't let him in. It was hilarious, I was, like, 'Dude, it's OK. He's Bob Dylan.'
>
> "When he came inside, he started pulling bits and pieces of paper out of his pockets, notes he took on the pad sitting next to the bed at whatever hotel he last stayed. He is one of America's greatest poets and still totally disorganized. He was one of the most charismatic, interesting people I've

ever met. When we were doing the song, I recorded him with just one microphone. He said, 'Man, I've been trying to record like this all my life.'"*

ELEANOR ROOSEVELT, 20 EAST 11TH STREET, LATER 21 WASHINGTON SQUARE WEST

Eleanor Roosevelt (1884–1962) was the wife of Franklin Delano Roosevelt, the four-term president of the United States. An active participant in the political process, Roosevelt also wrote newspaper columns, and was an American delegate to the United Nations.

JOHN SEBASTIAN, 3 WASHINGTON SQUARE SOUTH, AT BROADWAY

Sebastian was the lead singer and main songwriter for the folk-rock band The Lovin' Spoonful. He grew up in the Village, and his father, also named John Sebastian, was a world-class harmonica recitalist.

LINCOLN STEFFENS, SOUTH SIDE, WASHINGTON SQUARE

Steffens (1886–1936) was one of the pioneering muckraking journalists. He exposed political corruption and other wrongdoing in his book *The Shame of the Cities*.

BARBRA STREISAND, 64 WEST NINTH STREET

Streisand is a perpetually best-selling pop music artist, who has also had a successful career as an actress. In 1971, Dylan told Tony Glover that he originally wrote "Lay Lady Lay" for Streisand to record.

MARK TWAIN (SAMUEL CLEMENS), 14 WEST 10TH STREET

This is one of the residences of the great American humorist and novelist Twain (1835–1910).

---

*Ross Raihala, "Nile Rodgers Talks about Chic, Prince and His Doorman Mistaking Bob Dylan for the Unabomber," *Twin Cities Pioneer Press*, July 26, 2017, www.twincities.com/2017/07/26/nile-rodgers-talks-about-chic-prince-and-his-doorman-mistaking-bob-dylan-for-the-unabomber/.

EDGARD VARÈSE, 188 SULLIVAN STREET

Varèse (1883–1938) is sometimes known as the father of electronic music. Jazz saxophone player Charlie Parker was planning to study with him, but died before that was possible. Frank Zappa idolized his music and cited him as a major influence.

EDMUND WILSON, 114 WEST 16TH STREET

Edmund Wilson was an influential literary critic. This address is just north of Greenwich Village.

THOMAS WOLFE, HOTEL ALBERT, THEN 13 EAST EIGHTH STREET AND 263 WEST 11TH STREET

Like Theodore Dreiser, Wolfe (1900–1938) was regarded as a major novelist, but his reputation diminished as years went by. Wolfe was noted for turning in lengthy manuscripts, which were heavily edited by Maxwell Perkins.

86 GREENWICH AVENUE

86 Greenwich Avenue provided a home for a distinguished group of Village writers, including Djuna Barnes (1892–1982), Eugene O'Neill (1888–1953), John Reed (1887–1920), and Dorothy Day (1897–1980). Day was a journalist and social agitator who founded the radical Catholic Worker Movement.

East Village Residents

BÉLA BARTÓK, 350 BOWERY, CORNER OF GREAT JONES STREET

The great Hungarian composer (1881–1945) fled the Nazis and lived here during the 1940s.

WILLIAM S. BURROUGHS, 222 BOWERY

Home of the beat novelist Burroughs (1914–1997) during the 1970s. A legendary meeting occurred between Dylan and Burroughs in 1965. As Burroughs later told

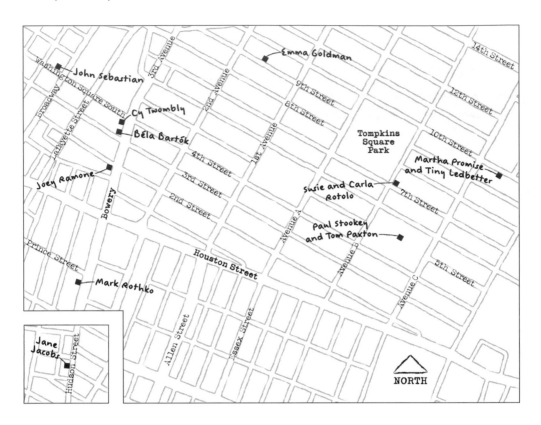

writer Victor Bockris, "he struck me as someone who was obviously competent. . . . If his subject had been something that I knew absolutely nothing about, such as mathematics, I would have still received the same impression of competence. Dylan said he had a knack for writing lyrics and expected to make a lot of money."*

EMMA GOLDMAN, 321 EAST NINTH STREET

Goldman (1869–1940) was a renowned anarchist leader and theoretician.

MARTHA PROMISE LEDBETTER AND TINY LEDBETTER, 414 EAST 10TH STREET

Martha Ledbetter (1904–1968), Lead Belly's widow, and his niece, Tiny (1923–2017), lived in this building between avenues C and D. On Tuesday nights Reverend Gary

---

*Victor Bockris, *With William Burroughs: A Report from the Bunker* (New York: St. Martin's Griffin, 1996).

Davis, famous for his guitar playing and his holy blues songs, would come down from his home in the Bronx to sing at Tiny's apartment. Tiny lived on the second floor, and as you entered the building, you could hear the music float magically down the stairwell. Gary's protégés and/or students include guitarists John Gibbon, Stefan Grossman, Ernie Hawkins, Barry Kornfeld, and many other guitarists active in the blues revival.

I once attended a party at Martha's house, where blues man John Lee Hooker confused Gary Davis with Lead Belly, who had been dead for some years. An embarrassing silence followed, interrupted by a competition-minded Gary Davis saying, "Mr. John Lee Hooker, I'll hook into you, and you'll hook into me."

39. Reverend Gary Davis performing at a house party with guitar, Dick Weissman to his right, and unidentified listeners, ca. 1959. Photo: Sound Associates. From the Ronald D. Cohen Collection #20239, Southern Folklife Collection, The Wilson Library, University of North Carolina at Chapel Hill.

JOEY RAMONE, SECOND STREET AND THE BOWERY

Joey (1951–2001) was the lead singer of the famous punk band The Ramones. Ramone first heard Dylan perform when his band was touring Japan in 1994. Stopping by backstage to say hello to Dylan's bass player, Ramone was surprised when Dylan walked in and greeted him warmly. He had no idea that Dylan knew his music.

MARK ROTHKO, HAD A STUDIO AT 222 BOWERY

Rothko (1903–1970) was one of the leading abstract expressionist painters of the twentieth century.

SUZE AND CARLA ROTOLO, AVENUE B AND SEVENTH STREET

In 1964 when Suze Rotolo (1943–2001) returned from Italy she moved into her sister Carla's (1941–2014) apartment. Suze had been Dylan's girlfriend and muse. She was an illustrator and painter. Carla was her older sister. She worked as an assistant for Alan Lomax and as a set designer.

PAUL STOOKEY AND TOM PAXTON, 629 EAST FIFTH STREET

Early home of the famous Village folk singers.

CY TWOMBLY, 356 BOWERY

Twombly (1928–2011) was a prominent painter, photographer, and sculptor.

Coda

So Much Dylan

Words and music by Dick Weissman, Longest Bridge Music, ASCAP, used by permission. From the album *Four Directions*. Can be heard at www.dickweissman.com.

He followed his thumb to New York town,
They said he was destined to wear the crown.
The gypsy woman told him he would be a star,
Ride in a limo with a private bar.
But there wasn't much Dylan, no not much Dylan.
CHORUS
No curtains in the kitchen, paintings in the hall,
Posters in the windows at the shopping mall,
Not enough Dylan,
To make you want to lose your mind.

The record deal came like he knew it would,
They were sorting through his garbage in the neighborhood,
Then good Queen Joan deigned to share her throne,
But soon she was sitting in a no-fly zone,
Without Bob Dylan, no there wasn't much Dylan.
CHORUS
Curtains in the kitchen, paintings in the hall,
Posters in the windows at the shopping mall,
So much Dylan, bound to make you lose your mind.

Blowin' in the wind, harmonica wailin',
I understand he's courtin' Sarah Palin,

He lay her cross his big brass bed,
He never did tell her, that he used to be a red,
So much Dylan, bound to make you lose your mind.
CHORUS
Curtains in the window, paintings in the hall,
Videos playing at the shopping mall,
So much Dylan, bound to make you lose your mind.
So much Dylan, bound to make you lose your mind.
(spoken) Too much Dylan!

Bob-liography

Note: The website of Powell's Books in Portland lists some three hundred books about Bob Dylan in stock, and about the same number that are out of stock. The books in this bibliography bear particular relevance to Bob Dylan and the Greenwich Village of the 1960s and early 1970s.

Block, Rory. *When a Woman Gets the Blues.* Location unlisted: Aurora Productions, 2011.

Cohen, John. *Young Bob: John Cohen's Early Photographs of Bob Dylan.* New York: Powerhouse Books, 2003.

Cunningham, Agnes "Sis," and Gordon Friesen. *Red Dust and Broadsides: A Joint Autobiography.* Amherst: University of Massachusetts Press, 1999.

Dalton, David. *Who Is That Man? In Search of the Real Bob Dylan.* New York: Hyperion, 2003.

Dylan, Bob. *Chronicles: Volume One.* New York: Simon & Schuster, 2004.

Dylan, Bob. *Tarantula.* New York: The Macmillan Company, 1971.

Gill, Andy. *Don't Think Twice, It's All Right: Bob Dylan, the Early Years.* New York: Thunder's Mouth Press, 1998.

Hadju, David. *Positively 4th Street: The Lives and Times of Joan Baez, Bob Dylan, Mimi Baez Farina, and Richard Fariña.* New York: North Pole Press, 2001.

Havens, Richie, with Steve Davidowitz. *They Can't Hide Us Anymore.* New York: Avon Books, 1991.

Heylin, Clinton. *Bob Dylan: A Life in Stolen Moments—Day by Day: 1941–1995.* New York: Schirmer Books, 1996.

Heylin, Clinton. *The Double Life of Bob Dylan: A Restless, Hungry Feeling (1941–1966).* New York: Little, Brown and Company, 2021.

Hoskyns, Barney. *Small Town Talk: Bob Dylan, The Band, Van Morrison, Janis Joplin, Jimi Hendrix & Friends in the Wild Years of Woodstock.* New York: Da Capo Press, 2016.

McKenzie, Peter. *Bob Dylan: On a Couch & Fifty Cents a Day.* New York: MKB Press, 2021.

Maymudes, Victor, co-written and edited by Jacob Maymudes. *Another Side of Bob Dylan: A Personal History on the Road and off the Tracks.* New York: St. Martin's Press, 2015.

Miller, Terry. *Greenwich Village and How It Got That Way*. New York: Crown Publishers, 1990.

Neff, Peter. *That's the Bag I'm In: The Life, Music and Mystery of Fred Neil*. Nashville: Blue Ceiling Publishing, 2019.

Petrus, Stephen, and Ronald D. Cohen. *Folk City: New York and the American Folk Revival*. Oxford: Oxford University Press, 2015.

Pickering, Stephen. *Bob Dylan Approximately: A Portrait of the Jewish Poet in Search of God: A Midrash*. New York: David McKay Company, 1975.

Rotolo, Suze. *A Freewheelin' Time: A Memoir of Greenwich Village in the Sixties*. New York: Broadway Books, 2007.

Santelli, Robert. *The Bob Dylan Scrapbook 1956–1966*. New York: Simon & Schuster, 2005.

Sawyers, June Skinner. *Bob Dylan: New York*. Berkeley: Roaring Forties Press, 2011.

Schumacher, Michael. *There But for Fortune: The Life of Phil Ochs*. Minneapolis: University of Minnesota Press, 2018

Shelton, Robert. *No Direction Home: The Life and Music of Bob Dylan*. New York: Beech Tree Press, 1986.

Strausbaugh, John. *The Village: 400 Years of Beats and Bohemians, Radicals and Rogues: A History of Greenwich Village*. New York: ECC, 2013.

Van Ronk, Dave, with Elijah Wald. *The Mayor of MacDougal Street: A Memoir*. New York: Da Capo Press, 2005.

Wald, Elijah. *Dylan Goes Electric!: Newport, Seeger, Dylan and the Night that Split the Sixties*. New York: Dey St., 2015.

Winn, John R. *"This Singin' Thing": Untold Tales of a Traveling Troubadour from the 1960's*. Location unlisted: E.R. Whipple Publishing, 2015.

Woliver, Robbie. *Hoot! A 25-Year History of the Greenwich Village Folk Scene*. New York: St. Martin's Press, 1994.

Wetzsteon, Ross. *Republic of Dreams: Greenwich Village: The American Bohemia, 1910–1960*. New York: Simon & Schuster, 2003.

Index